SPINNING AND WEAV

The prohibitive cost of spinning w
courage many prospective weavers, but this instructional guide
shows how to build your own low-cost equipment, clearly
explaining the techniques for turning a fleece into cloth.

Cover photograph by E. A. Longmore

£2.95

SPINNING AND WEAVING AT HOME

Expert Advice on Constructing and Using Your Own Low-cost Spinning Wheel and Loom

by
Thomas Kilbride

THORSONS PUBLISHERS LIMITED
Wellingborough, Northamptonshire

First published September 1980
Second Impression December 1981

British Library Cataloguing in Publication Data

Kilbride, Thomas
Spinning and weaving at home.
1. Hand spinning
2. Hand weaving
3. Woollen and worsted spinning
I. Title
746.1 TT847

ISBN 0-7225-0552-3
ISBN 0-7225-0551-5 Pbk

Typeset by Harper Phototypesetters, Northampton.
Printed and bound in Great Britain by
Weatherby Woolnough, Wellingborough, Northants
on paper made from 100% re-cycled fibre.

CONTENTS

INTRODUCTION

Fifty years ago, in this remote area of West Ross where I now live, every woman could spin. Many a long winter's night was spent spinning by the fire to produce the yarn for knitting or weaving. Spinning was not their main occupation, indeed for most it was a relatively minor one. But yarn was needed by everyone so everyone knew how to spin. It was taken for granted.

Towards Self-Sufficient Living

Today there is hardly a trace of what was, until recently, a routine but essential part of life. The knowledge and the necessary equipment have all but disappeared. The wheels have been burnt or destroyed by worm and most of the old-time spinners, thinking back to the tedium and the eye-strain, might well say 'Good riddance to bad rubbish'. That attitude certainly suits the spinner with his factory full of spinning frames and his warehouse full of thread. He is the expert and he has the knowledge. But he also has the power, and the greater his monopoly of the knowledge, the greater his power. He, therefore, has the power to produce yarns that suit *him* rather than the yarns that suit *you*.

This situation does not only apply to yarns. How many times have you gone into a shop in the last year to enquire about a particular article only to be told that it is either out of stock, unobtainable, or has been replaced by a new model? Quite often, I would guess. If we do not have the skill and knowledge to make the thing ourselves we simply have to do without. By losing the ability to produce the necessities of life we lose control over a major part of our lives. The experts take control!

Of course there have to be limits. We cannot expect to be able to make everything we might need, but the more the better. Keep control! And that is really what the self-sufficiency movement is about. It is, among other things, an anti-specialization movement. It is a power to the people movement and, at its fringes, a spin and weave your own cloth movement.

There will be other advantages to learning how to spin and weave. Perhaps you or one of your neighbours have a few sheep. What could be more satisfying than to do the whole job from beginning to end, from raising a lamb to wearing a coat that you have made from its fleece? Sheep get very bad press. They are not the stupid, troublesome creatures they are so often made out to be. Give them a bit of individual attention and you will find that they are individuals with individual personalities. Each is unique and, as you get to know them better, you will realize that each fleece is also unique. Some will be more suitable for your spinning and weaving than others. Like most things the more you learn, the more you will realize there is to learn. If you do not have any sheep but have the space, it is well worth considering purchasing a few.

Time and Cost

One thing that ought to be said at the outset is that spinning and weaving by hand are both time-consuming activities. If you cost your time you will find that it is a very expensive way of producing thread or cloth. If you consider it from a narrow economic standpoint then it makes little sense. But take a broader view of things and there is a lot to be said for it, not the least of which is that spinning and weaving by hand can be interesting, satisfying and fun.

But there is a snag and that, for most people, is the cost of equipment to do the job. If you have a look at catalogues from suppliers of spinning and weaving equipment you will see what I mean. Spinning wheels can cost anything from £50 to £100 and loom prices are now so high as to put off many an interested individual. Such prices just do not fit in with the idea of the simple life of self-sufficiency.

Do-It-Yourself

The idea of this book, then, is to give instructions on how you can make your own equipment. Compared with bought equipment the cost will be minimal. The designs are dictated more by the desire to keep things simple and cheap than by any aesthetic considerations. Beauty may be in the eye of the maker rather than the beholder but they *will* work, and that is what counts.

Provided you are not all thumbs you should have no trouble with the designs in the book. They are geared to the handyman rather than the cabinet-maker. You will need a variety of tools and a list of the ones I used will be found in *Useful Information* at the end of the book.

You will find this book divided into roughly two parts. The first part is concerned with spinning and you will find instructions for making and using a spindle, a gadget I call an Indian Head Spinner, a great wheel and a spinning wheel, made mainly from bicycle parts. The second part is concerned with weaving and there are plans for making two looms; one designed to sit on a table while in use, and the other a much larger one which stands on the floor on its own four feet. There is also a chapter which describes, very basically, how to put a warp on a loom and how to weave. This is, of necessity, very sketchy and only intended as a starter. Anyone with a deeper interest in weaving will want to get hold of a few books specializing in it. You will find some listed in the bibliography but there are many, many more, some of which will be sure to suit your particular interest.

There is also a list of suppliers of accessories that are specialized or difficult to make.

1
SPINNING

Spinning is the process of twisting fibres together to form a thread which is longer and stronger than the fibres of which it is comprised. The temperate areas of the globe are blessed with a great variety and quantity of fibres suitable for spinning into thread. These can be divided into two main groups: animal and vegetable.

Among the more commonly used animal fibres are the coats of sheep, goats, llamas, yaks, rabbits and the cocoons of silk worms. In the vegetable group are the fibres of cotton, flax, coconut, and nettles, to name but a few. Almost all these fibres need some preparation before they are in a condition to be spun into thread. Flax, for instance, needs to be put through a number of quite complicated steps before it is ready to be spun. Wool preparation, on the other hand, is relatively simple. But, whatever the fibre, preparation and hand-spinning of fibres is always a time-consuming business. Since the second half of the eighteenth century spinning has been mechanized and the machine can produce thread infinitely faster and therefore cheaper than by hand-spinning.

Why Bother?

The question that comes immediately to mind then is, 'Why bother to hand-spin at all?' One answer is that we should in order to produce a thread which is not commercially available. Machine spinning has several disadvantages. For example, machine spinning is organized on a large scale. You cannot take the five fleeces from your own sheep to a woollen mill and get them back as thread. Your fleece will be swallowed up to feed a hungry carding machine that deals in fifty fleeces at a time rather than five, and you will never again know which is which. If you want to have thread from your own fleeces you will have to produce it yourself.

Secondly, machine-spun yarn is, by its nature, consistent. Hand-spun yarn, no matter how carefully it is produced, has a certain variation in texture and size. These variations can be as subdued or pronounced as your skill permits but they will always be there and they will give unique and distinctive character to whatever you make with your yarn—a character which cannot be reproduced by machine.

Thirdly, hand-spinning can produce a yarn as varied in colour as the fleece that went into it. A fleece with black, brown and white patches can be spun into a thread with similar variations. Machine-spinning on the other hand will tend to reduce such a fleece to a uniform grey thread.

So, by hand-spinning it is possible to produce a kind of yarn that cannot be produced by machine. I would also add to that the pleasure and satisfaction that spinning can give you. It can be a wonderfully relaxing way of spending your evenings. Once you get the knack—and spinning, like riding a bicycle, is more of a knack than a skill—the rythmic repetitive action will have a calming effect on your spirit.

In this country I would guess that ninety per cent of all hand-spinning is done with wool and consequently I shall use it as the example for the chapters on spinning.

Fleece

A fleece is the protective coat of the sheep or goat. It has two ingredients—hair and wool. Hair tends to repel water and wool to absorb it. Primitive breeds of sheep, goats and some cattle have an outer covering of hair, like a waterproof thatch, and an inner layer of wool which acts as insulation. Selective breeding has, over the years, reduced the percentage of hair in a fleece until today the majority of breeds have a relatively small amount of hair, or kemp, in their coat.

Once a year, usually in the early summer, the coat of the sheep is cut off or shorn. This fleece is our starting point. You will find that the shearer has rolled it up for storage. Carefully unroll it

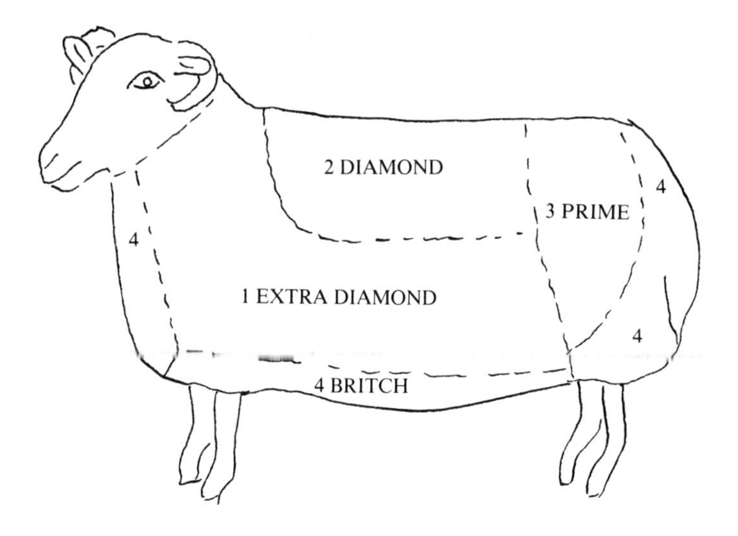

Figure 1. Sections of fleece graded according to quality.

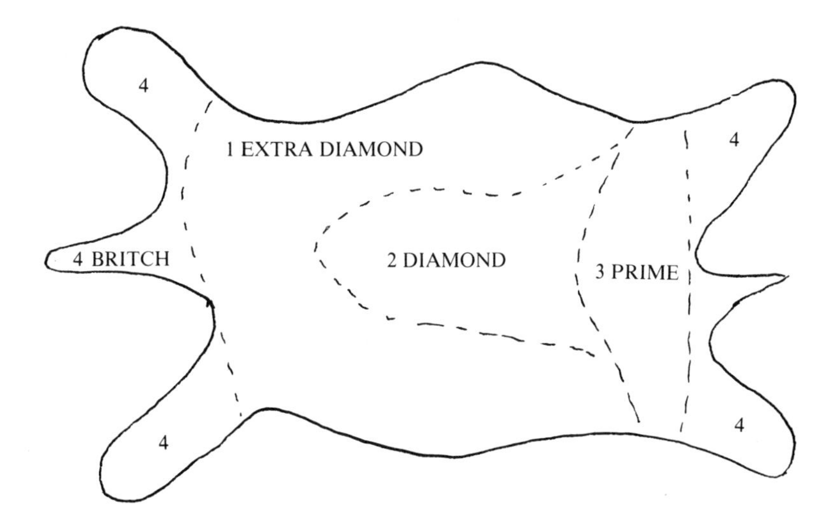

Figure 2. Position of graded sections of cut fleece.

and lay it flat on a clean floor. Get down on your hands and knees and have a good look at it. You will notice that different sections have different characteristics (see Figure 1). The position of a particular part on the body of the sheep accounts for much of that difference, some parts taking more weathering than others. The best sections are usually the sides and the back of the neck. Next, in order of merit, is the top back and, thirdly, the hind quarters. These three sections are usually designated extra diamond, diamond and prime. The pieces around the tail, feet and the front of the chest will be too dirty to use for hand-spinning and it is best to discard them (see Figure 3). There will also be overall differences between one fleece and another caused by the breed characteristics, the weather the animal has had to endure, and the quality of the feeding, particularly during the early spring. The variations possible are enormous and the best plan is to buy your first fleeces from someone who knows about hand-spinning and whom you know you can trust. Pull a lock of fibre from the centre of the fleece and you will be able to see the four main characteristics of a fleece. Firstly the length of the lock, secondly the thickness of each fibre in that lock, thirdly the amount of waviness in the lock and lastly the degree of shine or lustre on the fibre. These four qualities are usually referred to as staple, count, crimp and lustre, respectively.

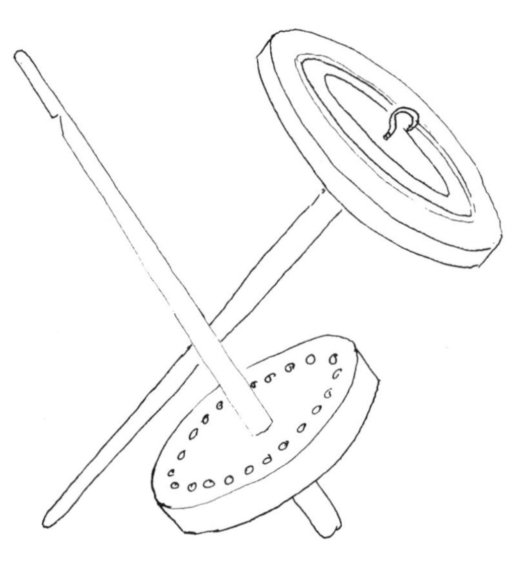

Figure 3. Two types of spindle.

Not all fleeces are suitable for the novice hand-spinner. Some, like the mountain breeds, have too high a proportion of kemp, or hair. Others, like many of the Downland breeds, produce a fleece which is too short for easy handling. As a general rule avoid the extremes of length, thickness or crimp. (A good quality Cheviot fleece might be a suitable starter.) Look out also for any thin or weak spots in the length of the lock. This will denote that the sheep was in poor physical condition some time during its fleece growing cycle and the fibres will tend to pull apart during the spinning process thereby weakening the thread.

You will find some more information about various breeds and their characteristics in Chapter 8, and a number of books which deal more fully with sheep and wool are mentioned in *Useful Information.*

2
SPINDLE SPINNING

Spindles have been around for a long time. They are the simplest of the gadgets designed to speed up the production of thread—the Ancient Egyptians and even Stone Age man used them. At the present time they are still quite widely used in Crete and Greece.

A spindle consists of a central stick with a circular weight or fly wheel attached near one end. Most peoples have used a spindle with the weight or whorl near the bottom, but the Egyptians did it the other way round, weight on top and stick extending down from it (Figure 3).

Making a Spindle

Figure 4 gives the specifications for making a spindle of medium size and weight suitable for spinning woollen thread. It is the type that has the weight at the bottom. As you can see, it is very simple—just two parts, the shaft and the whorl. For the shaft use a 250mm length of hardwood dowel, 10mm diameter. Sand it so that it tapers slightly from base to tip, 45mm from the tip cut a notch as illustrated in Figure 4. It should be 2mm deep or a third of the diameter of the shaft.

For the whorl use oak or a similar hardwood. From a piece 14mm thick cut an 80mm diameter circle, sand it down so that it is smooth and drill a 9mm hole through the centre. You should be able to slip the whorl down into the shaft. It should rest about 50mm from the bottom of the shaft. It may be necessary

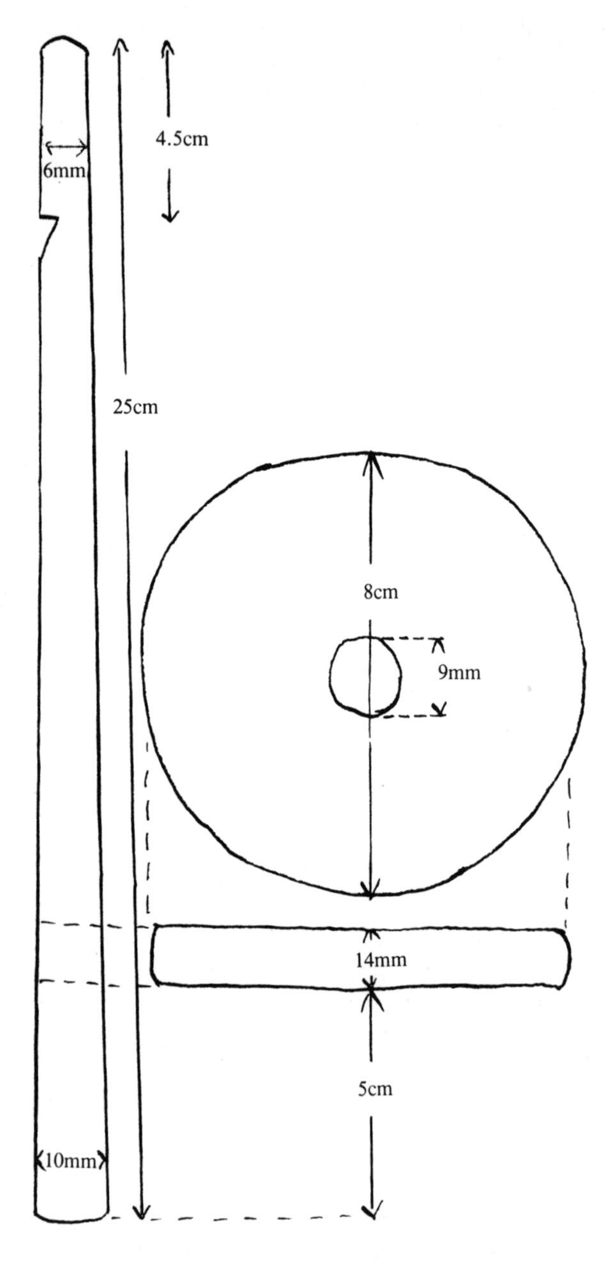

Figure 4. Traditional European Spindle with hardwood whorl and shaft.

to sand the shaft a bit more so that the whorl fits tightly at the correct height on the shaft. Finally, give it another sanding and two coats of clear varnish or wax polish. There is your spindle. You will be itching to get going but it will be worth your while to pause before you do and give some consideration to the theory of spinning.

Spinning Thread

Spinning is a three-stage operation and Figure 5 is intended to illustrate this. In the first stage the fibre to be spun is teased out into a light and fluffy mass. Dirt, extra short fibres, bits of brambles or bracken and the like are all sorted from the fleece and rejected. In most cases this fluffy mass is then combed or carded so that the fibres lie more or less parallel to each other. All this falls within the first part of the illustration—fibre preparations. Stage two involves pulling some of the fibres out of the fluffy mass of fibre and twisting them, or draughting as it is called, around each other to form a thread. The third stage is the storing of the thread produced.

It is possible to spin using only your hands. This exercise will help you understand what happens later when you start to use the spindles and wheels you will make. Take hold of a lock of fleece by the tips and with the other hand loosen and tease it into a light and fluffy mass. Reject any bits of dirt or vegetable

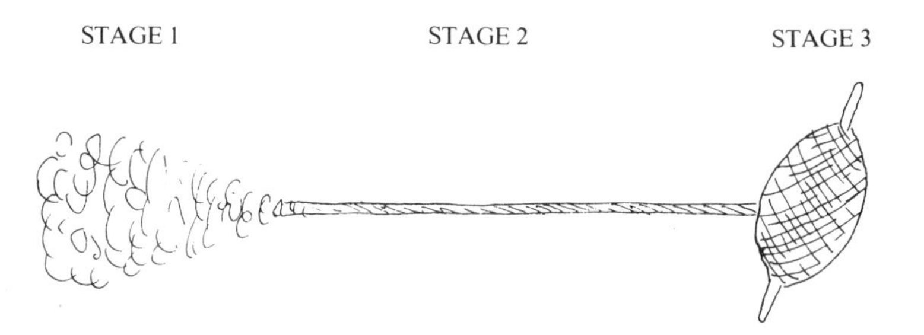

Figure 5. The three stages of spinning.

matter. Then, holding this mass of fibres in one hand, draw some of the fibres away from it, twisting them with the other hand in a clockwise direction as you pull them out. This will form a thread. As you pull away with the twisted thread the fibres will tend to catch onto other fibres in the store and they, in their turn, will be pulled into the evolving thread. When you have about 15cm of thread between your hands wind it into a ball that can be tucked away in your palm and start the pulling and twisting sequence again.

Using Your Spindle

Now, although this may be a fine way of demonstrating the principles of spinning, it is a rather inefficient way of producing thread. Obviously, if you want to make any quantity of yarn more efficient alternatives will have to be found for all three stages of the operation just described.

And this is where the spindle comes in. It may be the simplest of the spinning gadgets but it is a great improvement on finger spinning. Before starting to spin, a length of two-ply thread about 70cm long should be tied to the shaft of the spindle near to the whorl. This thread should be taken down, around the base of the shaft and then back up to the notch where a half-hitch secures it to the top of the shaft (see Figure 6). This is called the leader. It is just to get you started and will give you something to fix onto when you do start. Fluff out the end of this thread or leader to assist it to get a grip on the fibres to be spun.

Tease out a bundle of fibres into a light and fluffy mass and place the fluffed out end of the leader among them. With the right hand give the spindle, which is hanging suspended from the leader, a clockwise twist. The twist will run up the leader into the fibres, first joining the leader to the fibres, and then beginning to spin the fibres in your hand into a thread. Pinch the thread at the top of the leader with your right hand and pull away from your left hand thereby thinning out the fibres into a sliver thin enough for spinning into a thread. Run your right hand up this thin sliver; the twist generated by the twisting spindle will follow your right hand up and will spin the fibres into a thread. Pull some more fibres out from the fibre mass and start the process again. If the spindle loses its momentum and stops rotating give it another twist with the right hand and then take it back up the thread to ease fibres out of the mass in the left hand, allowing the twist to run up and make them into a thread.

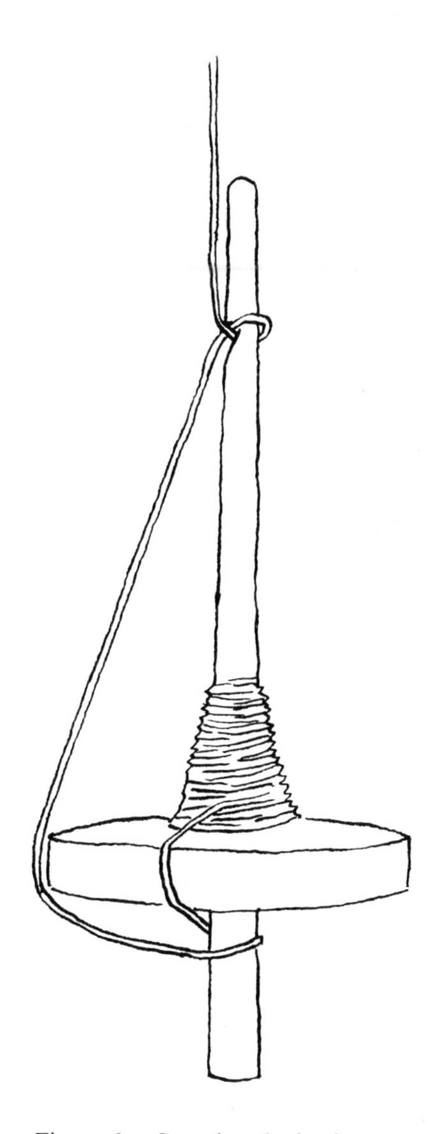

Figure 6. Securing the leader.

By the time you have spun about a metre you will find it difficult to reach down to twist the spindle. The time has come to wind on. First collect the spun thread in a butterfly on the thumb and first finger of your left hand and undo the half-hitch with which the leader is attached to the top of the spindle shaft. Unwind the leader also from the bottom of the shaft below the whorl, and then proceed to wind the thread from your left hand onto the spindle just above the whorl. When you have about 30cm of thread between your hands, refix the thread to the spindle as before and recommence the spinning process. With a little practice you will find that you can wind the spun thread and refix in a very few seconds.

As you spin the store of thread will grow and the store of fibres in your left hand will shrink. When you have used up all the fibres in your left hand fluff out some more and start again. It may take you some time to get the knack, but persevere. In my experience children pick it up much quicker than adults, but once you have got it you can call yourself a spinner, or spinster if you prefer.

Advantages of the Spindle

Spinning with the spindle is not as tedious as it might at first appear. It has some distinct advantages. A spindle can be tucked away in a pocket or bag and is light to carry—unlike its more efficient relative, the spinning wheel. It is also a good deal cheaper. On the other side of the balance is the fact that it is certainly slow. Once you get the knack, however, you can get along surprisingly fast. Its portability was one of its main advantages in the past for it was possible to herd cows or sheep and to spin at the same time, a practice which still persists in some areas of the world to this day.

3
THE GREAT WHEEL

The great wheel was probably the first innovation in the spinning field after the spindle. Its history is a bit uncertain but it seems to have cropped up first in the East. Basically, it is a spindle turned on its side with a pully substituted for the whorl. This pully is connected to a large wheel by a drive belt. The main advantage is that the spindle can rotate very fast. This is made possible by the difference in size between the great wheel and the pully wheel. This means faster twisting and easier storage of the spun thread. The whole operation becomes much more efficient, but it has its disadvantages too. A wheel cannot be carried around in the pocket like a spindle and so, historically, it is linked with the development of more or less static living arrangements. The nomadic peoples, the herders and the very primitive groups stuck to the spindle which was better suited to their way of life. The wheel goes with the establishment of permanent human settlements and the larger houses which followed.

Efficient Teasing

As I have said the wheel makes it possible to produce yarn much faster than the spindle and this increase in speed brings with it certain complications, the most important of which is the need for a more efficient way of fluffing out or teasing the fleece ready for feeding it to the wheel. This process, a refinement of the teasing that you did to the fleece to be used for spindle spinning, is called carding. Figure 7 shows a pair of cards. As you can see they are flat, or in some cases, slightly dished, wooden paddles with metal pins protruding from one face. The pins are, in fact, set in a leather or synthetic base which is, in its turn, attached to the card.

Carding is a relatively modern method of preparing fleece. The technology to produce cheaply great quantities of metal pins did not evolve until the 1700s and it is unlikely that hand cards were widespread much before 1750. Prior to this time, combing was used to prepare the fibres where a particularly fine thread was required, but the majority of thread was probably spun from fleece which had just been teased. It is sometimes suggested that teazles were used to card fleece prior to the introduction of metal-pinned cards. I doubt if this was ever done on a large scale. Anyone who has tried teazles for carding will know that in use they quickly lose the tiny hooks on the ends of their arms and as a result lose their ability to get a grip of the fleece. My guess is that the widespread use of cards coincided with the introduction of the fly shuttle loom with its increased demand for yarn. Prior to that almost all thread was spun from

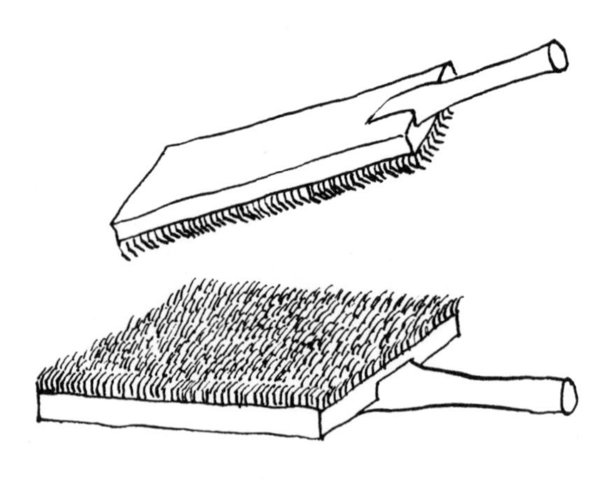

Figure 7. A pair of cards.

hand-teased fleece. Metal-pinned cards answered the demand for an increase in the speed and efficiency of fleece preparation, and they still do so. Today, cards are easily available and although somewhat expensive they are the very devil to make. If you take my advice you will buy a pair.

Carding

Carding is one of those activities which can be taught by example in about five minutes but which takes a chapter of words to describe. If you have any friends who are spinners get them to show you how to card. Example followed by experience are, as in most things, the best teacher. If that is not possible the following will be a poor substitute.

The object of carding is to line up the fibres of the fleece you intend to spin so that they are parallel to each other. Carding should be done sitting down. The cards are held one in each hand with the sets of pins facing each other. The bottom card should have its handle away from you and the top one its handle towards you. The top card is the worker card, the bottom one just lies there, the passive card. With the top card, which is the one that does all the work, brush the fleece as you would brush your hair, that is, always in the same direction, towards you. You will find that the fleece gradually gets straightened out and forms itself into fringes trailing from the edge of each card. There are two points to watch: Firstly, keep the cards just brushing past each other. Do not let the pins bite into each other or it will become very hard work and the fibres will become embedded deep down in the pins. The cards should be moving past each other on parallel paths with a minute gap between the two layers of pins. Secondly, avoid making too long a stroke. Start the pull with the leading edge of the top card slightly short of the trailing edge of the bottom card. If this is not done you will find that the fleece tends to hook around the first row of pins rather than forming a fringe trailing from the last few rows. You will also lose a lot of skin from the knuckles of the hand holding the bottom card!

When most of the fibres have been transferred from the top to the bottom card clear the fibres from the bottom card and back onto the top card. Do this by holding both cards with their handles towards you and scrape the one card past the other in the opposite direction to that used in carding. The fibres will all have been cleared off the top card and you can start the whole business again. Repeat the process until the fibres lie on the cards in a light fluffy formation like well-brushed hair. Clear the fibres off the cards altogether. Do this by repeatedly using the clearing motion from one card back to the other until the fibres are clear of the pins. You will find that in doing so you have formed the fibres into a sausage-shaped roll called a rolag or roving. It will be a light, airy mass of wool with each fibre curled around the centre rather like the fibres in a silk-worm cocoon. This is carded fleece and is what you will feed to the spinning machines you will build.

MAKING A GREAT WHEEL

The Base

The wheel consists of three sections, the base with its four angled legs, the wheel and wheel support and the pulley and pulley

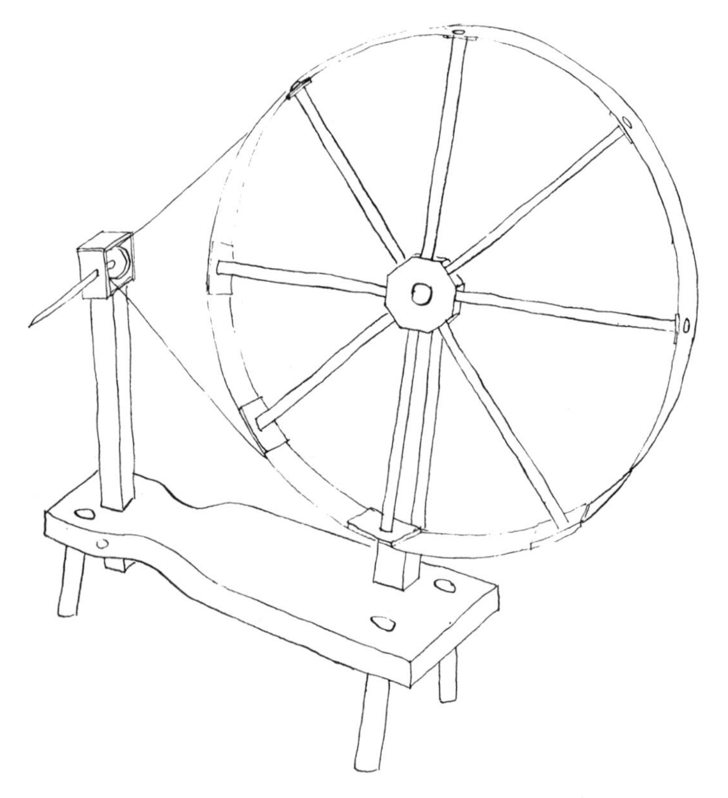

Figure 8. The Great Wheel.

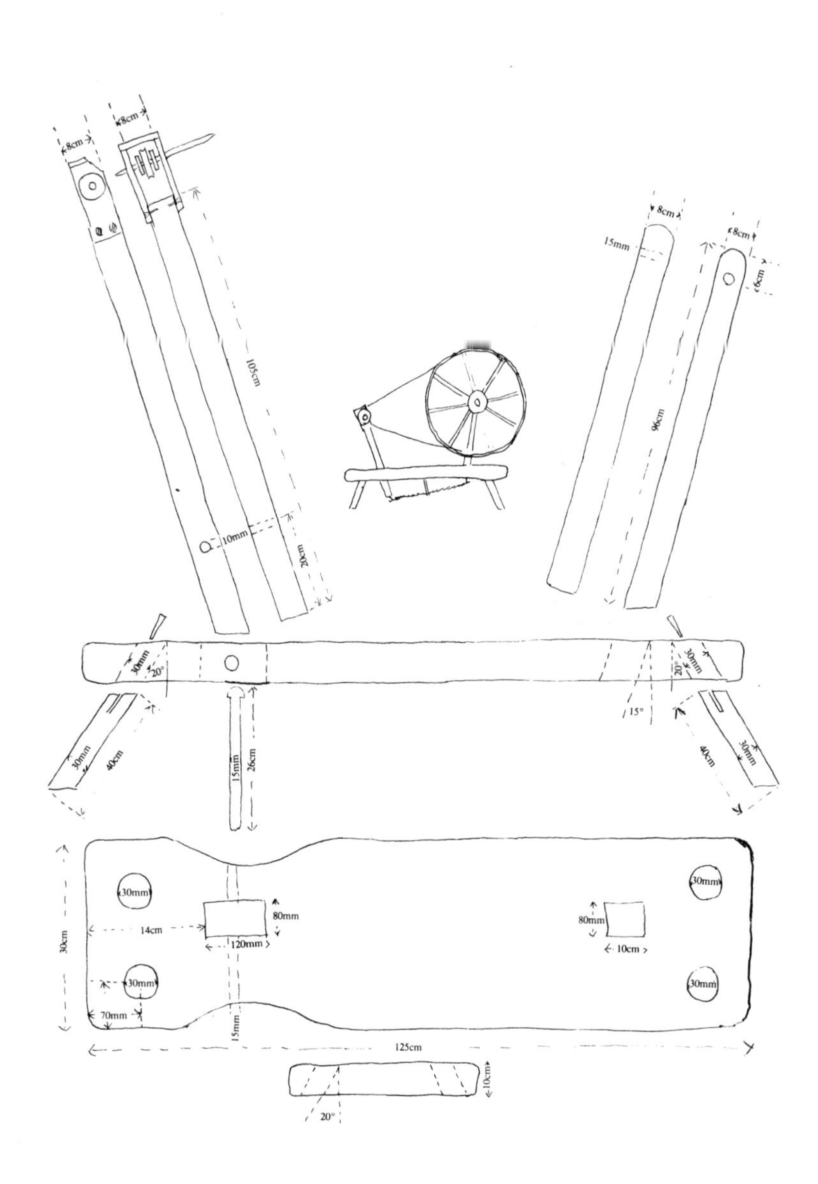

Figure 9a. The Great Wheel showing dimensions of base, pulley and wheel supports.

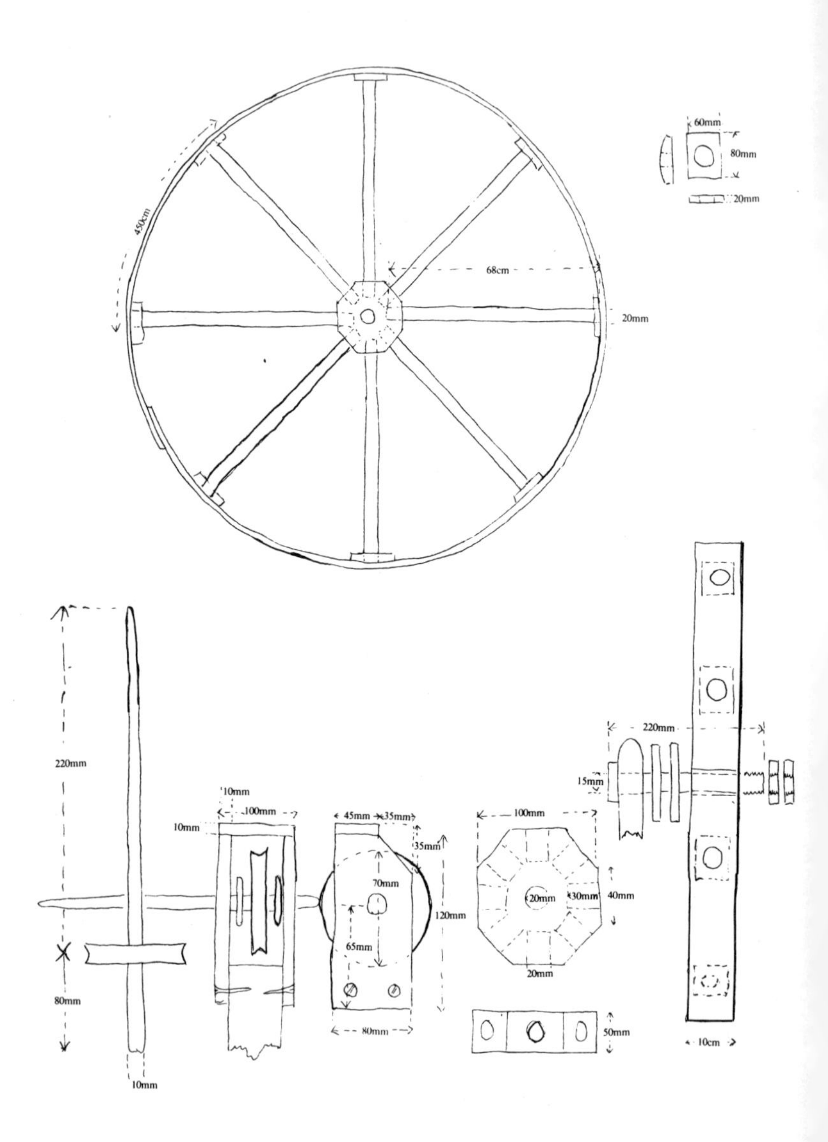

Figure 9b. The Great Wheel showing specifications for pulley and hub assemblies.

support. Have a good look at the sketch of a wheel (see Figure 8) and at the whole-page diagrams (Figures 9a and 9b). You should begin by making the base. It is made from a block of wood 125cm × 30cm × 10cm. What you use will depend on what you can get in this rather hefty size but something like parana pine would do very well. Cut it to size and shape out the 'waist' with a coping saw and round surform.

Next, cut out the holes to take the wheel support and pulley support. The easiest way to do this is to drill four small holes at the corners of the square and then cut from one hole to another round the four sides of the square with a coping saw. Square out the corners with a chisel. The pulley support hole is 80mm × 120mm and is not designed to be a tight fit on the pulley support. The support fits through the hole, protruding 20cm from the bottom and will be supported on a wooden rod which passes through the holes to be drilled in the base block and pulley support. The support can then pivot on the wooden rod. Drill a 15mm hole right through the base block (as shown in Figure 9a) making sure that it passes through the centre of the pulley support hole. This will require some care as you will probably have to drill in from each side, the drill itself being too short to do it in one operation. Make sure the two halves of the hole line up with each other. Cut out the hole for the wheel support 80mm × 80mm. Use the same system you used for the pulley support. You will notice that it is a sloping hole to allow the support to pitch forwards 15°. By drawing out the slope on the side of the block you should be able to drill and cut it accurately enough.

The Legs

Next, drill holes for the legs, 30mm diameter holes, also set at an angle. The holes should be drilled 20° off square in two directions—that is, they will slope out towards the corner. You will find it a help to drill a small pilot hole first as it is difficult to drill large holes at an angle. For the legs cut four 40cm lengths of 30mm dowel and make an 80mm saw cut from one end down the length of the leg. Glue the split ends of the legs into the base and drive a thin wedge into the saw cut from the top to make them firm. After the glue has dried trim off the tops and bottoms of the legs so that the base sits firmly on the ground.

The Pulley Support and Wheel Support

The pulley support should now be cut (8cm × 8cm × 105cm)

with a 15mm hole drilled through its centre 20cm from the bottom. Next, make the spindle. You will need a 70mm diameter pulley wheel with a 10mm hole through it and a 30mm length of 10mm steel rod. The pulley wheel can be obtained through an electrical or machine tool merchant or, if you are lucky, an ordinary hardware shop. With a file put a gradual taper on one half of the rod so that is approximately one half its original diameter at the tip. Slide the pulley onto the other end and fix it to the rod with Araldite 80mm from the unfiled end.

To hold the spindle in place on its support you will need to cut and assemble the three pieces which make up the pulley assembly. The two side pieces are 80mm × 120mm × 10mm with a corner cut off as in Figure 9b. Drill a 13mm hole through the centre of each side piece 65mm from the bottom. This hole should be lined with a 10mm length of steel or brass pipe with an inside diameter of 10mm and an outside diameter of 13mm to minimize the wear from the rotating spindle. Stick the lining into the hole with Araldite and allow to set. Slide the side pieces onto either end of the spindle and drill and screw the sides onto the support. You will notice that the spindle has considerable sideways movement. Remove one side piece again and slide washers onto either end of the spindle until this movement is reduced to about 5mm. Refix the sides. This time glue them into position. Cut the top piece of the assembly (10mm × 100mm × 45mm) and drill, nail and glue it in position. Finally, place the whole assembly into its hole in the base and support it in place by inserting a 25cm length of 15mm dowel through base and support.

Next cut the wheel support. It should be 8cm × 8cm × 96cm. Bore a 15mm hole through it 6cm from the top and fix the support into the base using the same method you used for the legs. If you find that the fit is not as tight as you might like, drive additional wedges into the edges of the hole around the support from the bottom until the support is firm.

Making the Wheel

You are now ready to make the wheel. First the rim. For this you will need two pieces of 3mm plywood 10cm × 235cm. Using a resin type glue, fix the two pieces together into one long strip allowing a 10cm overlap. Let this dry and then glue the two ends together with a similar overlap to make a circle. This is the rim. Next you will need eight blocks of wood, each 80mm × 60mm

× 20mm. In the centre of the piece drill a 20mm hole. It would be wise to hold the block in a vice while drilling these holes to prevent the blocks splitting. Each of these blocks needs one of its flat sides rounded with a surform so that it will fit snugly on the inside of the rim. Glue four of these blocks to the rim at the north, south, east and west positions.

Next, make the hub block. This is a block of hardwood 100mm × 100mm × 50mm with the four corners cut off to make it into an octagon. Drill a central hole 20mm in diameter to take the spindle and line it with a 50mm length of steel or brass tube of 20mm outside diameter and 15mm inside diameter. Next drill eight holes, one in each of the eight outer sides to take the spokes of the wheel. These should be 30mm deep and 20mm diameter. As before it is advisable to drill pilot holes with a small drill first. From 20mm dowel or broom handle cut 8 spokes each 68cm long.

To assemble the wheel lie the rim flat on the floor, fit the eight spokes into the hub and then lay the hub and spokes inside the rim. Fit four of the spokes into the holes on the spoke support blocks already fixed to the rim. Slide the other four blocks onto the remaining spokes and position them on the inside of the rim. The hub, spokes and rim should all fit snugly together. If the rim is loose on the spokes, put an equal piece of packing in the base of all the holes in the hub, sufficient to make the rim fit tightly. If, on the other hand, the rim is too tight, shave down all the spokes an equal amount until it fits. Once you have the wheel parts fitted together to your satisfaction, take them apart and glue the whole assembly together once more. While it is drying you will need to raise the hub 25mm off the floor in order to get it centred properly in the rim. The wheel can now be mounted on its support with a 15mm steel bolt 220mm long. The bolt should be held in place in the support with Araldite and the wheel held on the bolt with two nuts. Sufficient washers should be inserted between wheel and support so as to keep the wheel from rubbing on the supports as it revolves.

Connecting the Drive Wheel

To connect the drive wheel to the pulley you will need a 4½m length of strong linen or cotton cord which should be spliced, sewn or stuck into a continuous band, long enough to go around both wheel and pulley. (A friend tells me that the Post Office use a beautiful waxed linen thread in some of their cables!) Screw a large screw-eye into the bottom of the pulley support and another into the bottom of the wheel support, both beneath the base. Connect them with a loop of cord and, with the aid of a 100mm length of 7mm dowel, twist the loop until the tension on the drive band is as you want it. Keep the twist in the tension loop by wedging the dowel against the underside of the base. There you have it! All the wheel needs now is a good sandpapering and coat of varnish or wax. Try them both out on the underside of the base to see which you prefer. A drop of oil on the wheel and spindle bearings will not only help reduce friction, it will also reduce wear and save you having to replace the bearings too often.

Once you have had enough of admiring your handiwork it will be time to start spinning.

Working the Great Wheel

The Great Wheel is worked standing up—the right hand turns the wheel while the left hand feeds and controls the fibres being twisted into a thread. Connect a one-metre length of thread to the spindle to act as a leader just as you did with the hand spindle. Hold this leader in your left hand and give the wheel a clockwise turn with your right. By holding the thread in your left hand at just the right angle (about 140° from the spindle) you will find you can put a tension on the yarn without it pulling off the end of the spindle and that, at the same time, the twist from the spindle will travel up the leader. This will give you the combination of twist and tension needed to make a thread out of a bundle of fibres.

Now take a rolag in your left hand and allow some of the twist you have accumulated in the leader to run up into the fibres of the rolag and join it to the leader. Once joined you can draw out the fibre supply in the left hand while steadily twisting the wheel with the right. When you have spun about a metre of thread, move your left hand in towards the wheel. The thread will then be wound onto the spindle. Move your left hand away from the wheel again and you can start the sequence of drawing out the fibres and twisting them into a thread once again. Build up the thread on the spindle into a tapered cone (Figure 10) which, when large enough, should be wound off into a skein. Do not try slipping the whole cone off the end of the spindle. It will almost certainly end up an almighty tangle! The size and strength of the yarn you spin will be determined by how thinly you draw out the fibre supply and then how much twist you allow to bind the fibres together. With a little practice you will find you are able to judge the amount of drafting and twisting necessary to produce the thread you require.

Twisting the wheel clockwise will give a thread with a clockwise twist. This is usually referred to as 'Z' twist. You will find that the great majority of yours are 'Z' twist. Yarn twisted in the other direction is called 'S' twist (see Figure 11). Spinning 'S' twist yarn on a great wheel is not easy. The anti-clockwise spinning of the wheel is awkward. The best solution is to connect the drive band in a figure of eight thus reversing the direction of twist on the spindle while keeping the clockwise twist of the wheel (Figure 11).

Although using a great wheel continuously all day is very tiring—people used to say in the Scottish Highlands that it was the same as walking twenty miles—it is a great improvement on the hand spindle and with practice can become an efficient and pleasant way of producing yarn for knitting or weaving.

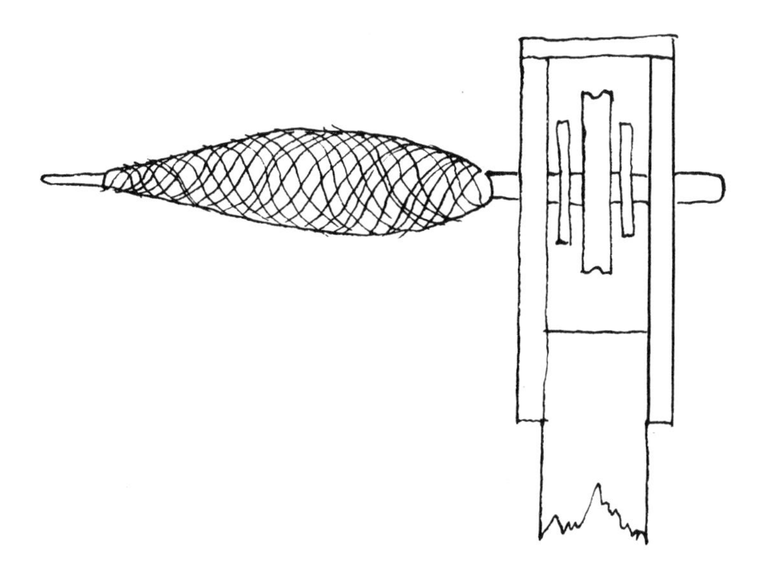

Figure 10. The thread built up on the spindle.

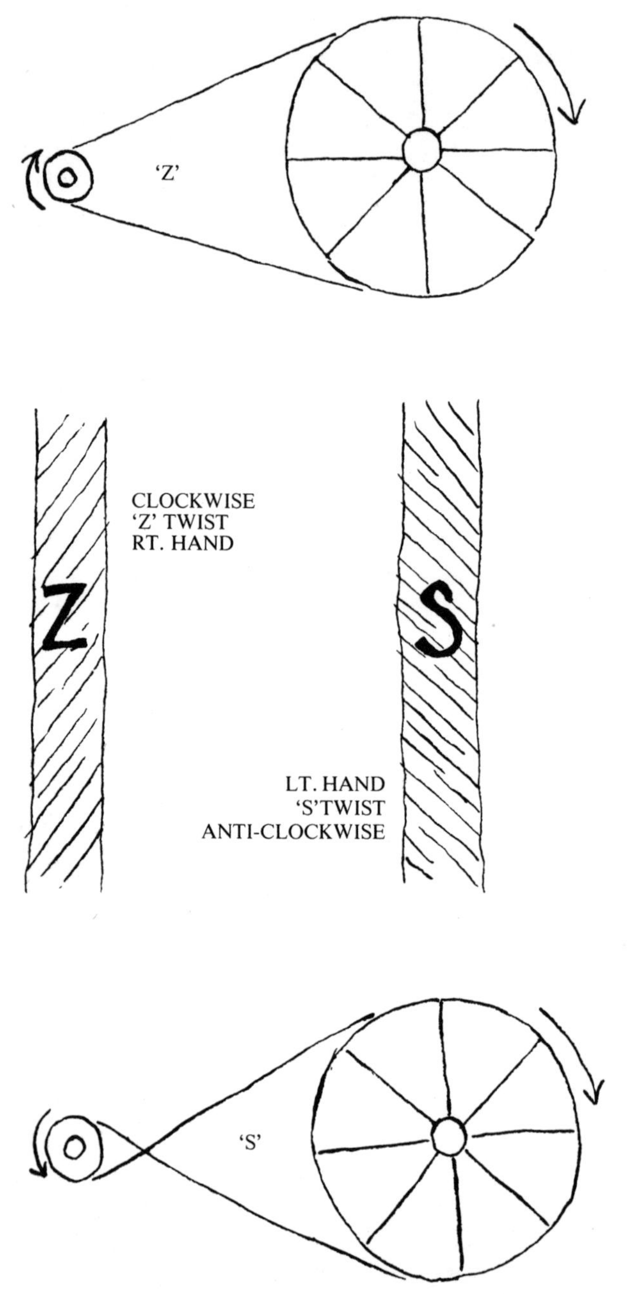

Figure 11. Clockwise ('Z') and anti-clockwise ('S') thread twist.

4
THE INDIAN HEAD SPINNER

In the preceding chapters I dealt with two simple methods of making a thread; the first using a spindle, the second using a Great Wheel. Both have an attractive simplicity about them but hand in hand with this characteristic goes one main disadvantage. The process of producing thread is an intermittent one; first you twist, then you store, then you twist and so on. Consequently it is a slow business.

In about 1490 Leonardo da Vinci invented a gadget which dramatically increased the speed at which thread could be produced. It did not come into general use in Europe for another seventy years or so and when it did the idea was credited to a German called Johann Jurgen. It quickly spread and the principles involved laid the foundations of the machine spinning industry which eventually followed. Its crucial characteristic was that it allowed the twisting and storing of a thread to be done concurrently and so allowed spinning to become a continuous process.

The Home-made Spinner

The Indian Head Spinner which will be described in this chapter uses da Vinci's principle of concurrent twisting and storing. It is a rather hefty spinner and is designed for producing rather hefty yarns suitable for knitting sweaters or weaving rugs. Figure 12 is a drawing of an Indian Head Spinner and Figures 13a, 13b, 13c and 13d show the three parts of which it is comprised.

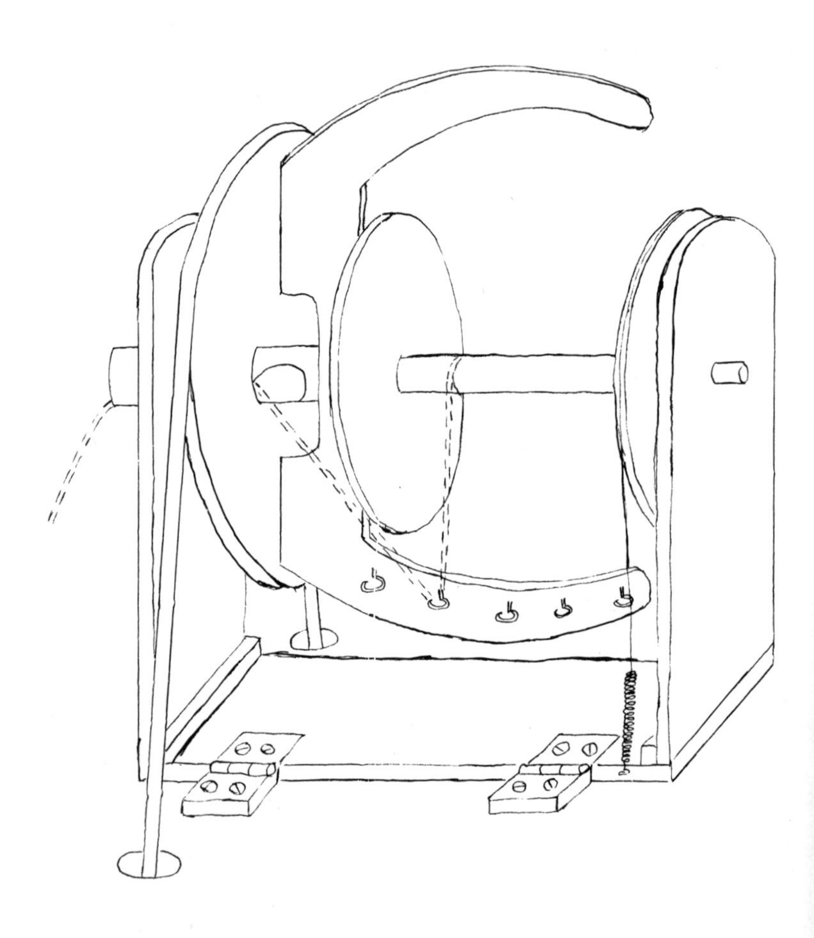

Figure 12. The Indian Head Spinner.

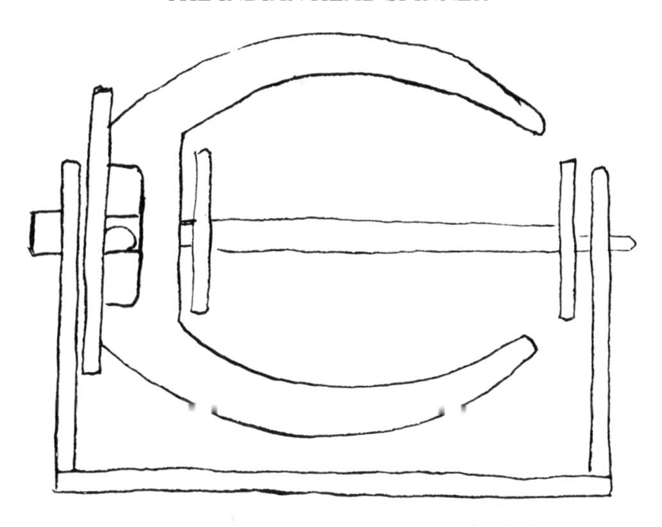

Figure 13a. The Indian Head Spinner in cross section.

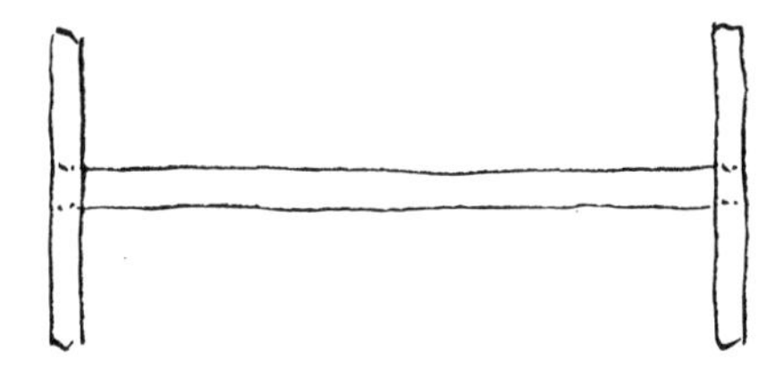

Figure 13b. The bobbin.

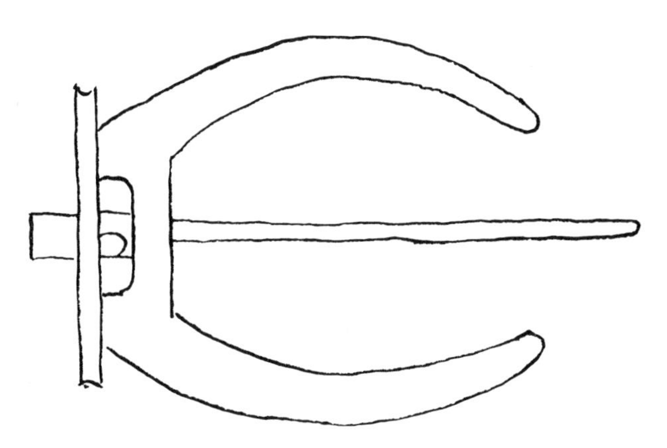

Figure 13c. The flyer and drive pulley.

The Indian Head Spinner is intended to be used with an old sewing machine base which provides the power, so acquiring of one of these is the first task. At one time there were a great many different models available. Singer were, of course, the best known but there were many others. Made of cast iron and wood and beautifully decorated in black and gold to match the sewing machines that stood on them, they are almost works of art. All have a treadle that is rocked back and forth using both feet and the drive is transferred to the machine or, in your case, the spinner, by a continuous drive band. Some have a well in the top in which the spinner will sit. Others have a hinged top allowing the machine to be swung down into the body of the treadle for storage. This type does not have a well, their top is flat, as they were designed to be used as a table when the machine was swung away, but both types can be adapted for use as a spinner base. As you will have noticed from Figure 13a, the spinning head is made up of three parts—a base, a flyer and a bobbin—and I suggest you make them in that order.

The Base

The base is made of either 12mm ply or similar size hardwood board. As you will see from Figure 14 the bottom is 220mm × 140mm × 12mm. The sides are both the same size—140mm × 160mm × 12mm with the top corners rounded. Drill the two end-pieces to take the spindle—one end with a small hole to take the thin end, the other with a larger one to take the thick end. Both holes should have a short (12mm) length of steel or nylon pipe as a lining to minimize wear. Thus, the exact size of the holes will depend on the outside measurement of the pipe you

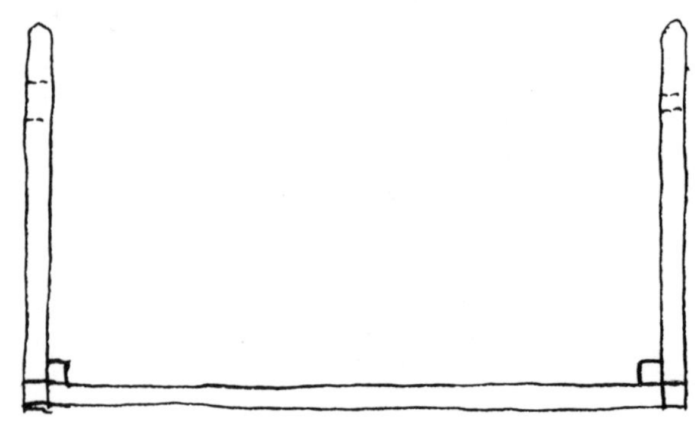

Figure 13d. The base.

find to use as a liner. The inside diameter should be 7mm and 20mm respectively and each hole should be centred 120mm from the base of the side. Glue the liners into the sides with Araldite. Now glue one of the sides onto the base with woodworkers glue as in Figure 14, gluing in an additional piece of wood 140mm × 15mm × 15mm on the inside of the corner to act as a strengthener. Drill and pin into this piece from the sides and the bottom using 30mm panel pins. Use a set square to ensure the side is at right angles to the base. Allow glue to dry, sand and varnish. The other side will be fitted to the base in similar fashion when the flyer and bobbin have been made.

The Flyer and Drive Pulley

The flyer and its drive pulley (see Figure 13c) are a little more difficult. The pulley wheel is cut from 12mm ply. Cut two circles, one with a 120mm diameter, the other a 40mm diameter. With a 1/32-inch drill bit, drill a central hole in each circle, slip them both onto a nail, and stick them together with wood glue as in Figure 15b. When the glue is set, drill a 20mm hole through both pieces of wood, taking care to keep it central and straight. The 1/32-inch pilot hole will help you do this but large holes in ply do tend to wander off to one side or another so—beware!

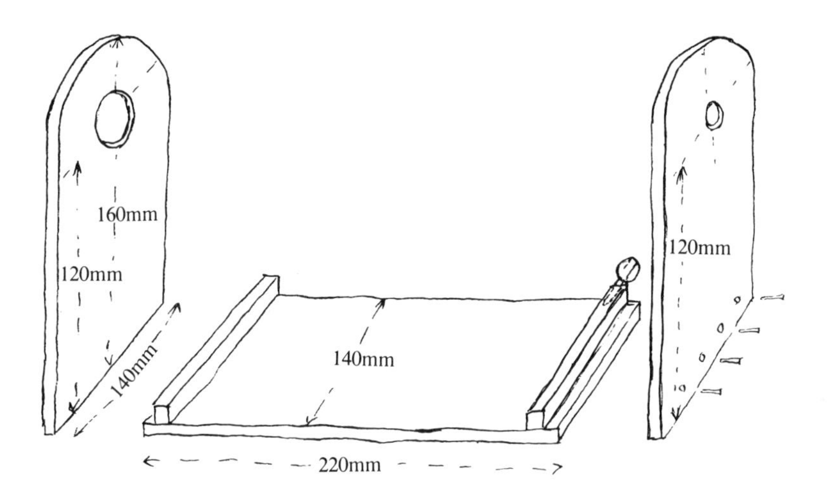

Figure 14. The base and sides of the Indian Head Spinner.

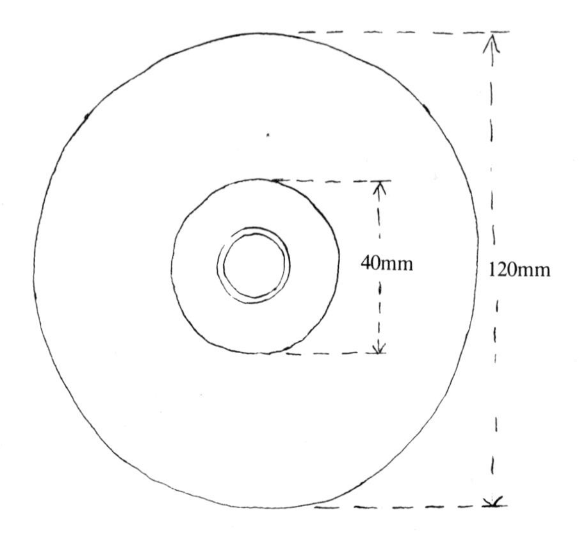

Figure 15a. The pulley wheel (front view).

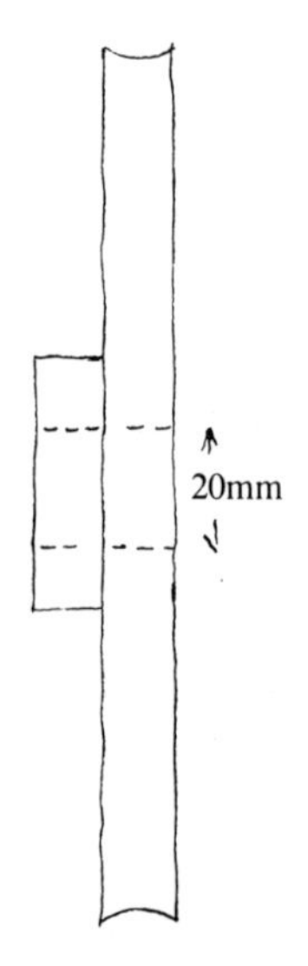

Figure 15b. The pulley wheel (side view).

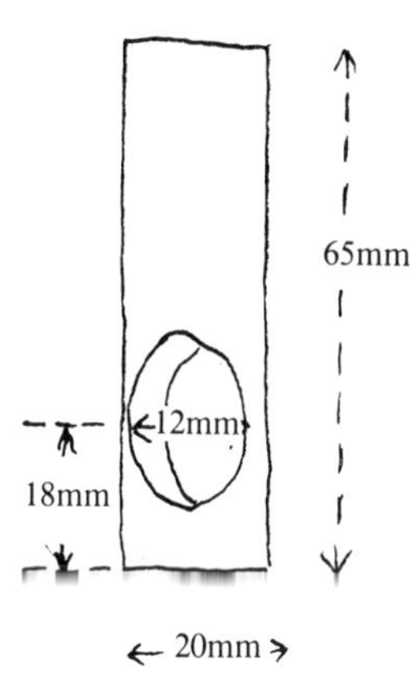

Figure 16a. The position of the holes in the pulley wheel pipe.

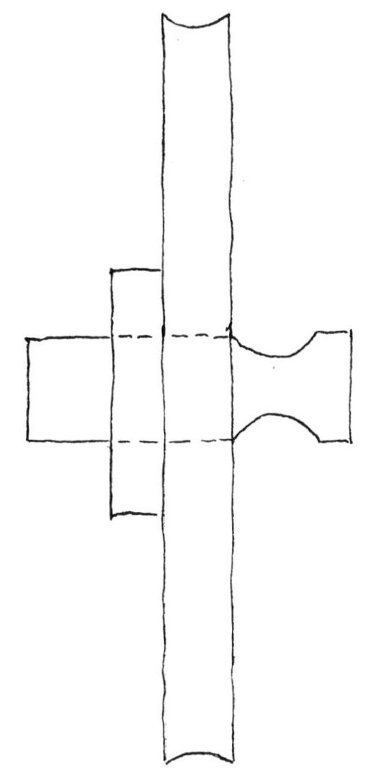

Figure 16b. The fixed position of the pipe through the pulley wheel.

Next, cut a 65mm length of steel pipe with an outside diameter of 20mm. Two holes must be made in the sides of the pipe, as shown in Figure 16a. The two holes, which are directly opposite each other on either side of the pipe are 12mm in diameter and are centred 18mm from one end of the pipe (see Figure 16a). Use a round file to make the holes and be sure to smooth off the sides. The spun thread passes through these holes on its way to the bobbin and so it is important that there are no sharp edges. This length of pipe is now ready to set in the wooden pulley wheel as in Figure 16b. With your round surform enlarge the diameter of the pulley centre hole until the metal pipe is a snug fit. Apply a liberal quantity of Araldite to the inside of the hole and slide the hole into position as shown in Figure 16b. The holes in the sides of the pipe should be just clear of the pulley wheel, that is, the pipe should extend 24mm.

The flyer is now cut from 12mm ply. Its pattern is shown half-size in Figure 17a so you should redraw it to twice the size. Make a tracing of the pattern, trace onto the ply sheet and cut it out, with a coping saw. Sand off all the edges. The central spindle is a 6mm steel rod 175mm long. Drill a 6mm hole in the centre of the flyer as shown in Figure 17b. Line the hole with Araldite and slide in the rod allowing 12mm to protrude as shown in Figure 17a. When all glue is set the flyer and the pulley are ready to be joined together (see Figure 18). Note that the flyer and pulley have to be set in exactly the right relationship to each other. Hold the pulley wheel with the plain end of the pipe away from you. Mark two points on the pulley wheel 15mm in from the circumference, so placed that if they are at 12 o'clock and 6 o'clock then the holes in the sides of the pipe point to 1.30 and 7.30. Drill $^{1}/_{32}$-inch hole through these points. Now line up the flyer on these points (Figure 18), pin and glue taking care that flyer and pulley wheel are at right angles to each other. You will notice that the flyer spindle protrudes into the end of central pulley pipe but that it does not fit tightly. Fill this space with plastic padding mixed up and applied according to the makers instructions. This will give the whole assembly additional rigidity and strength. When all glues have set cut a groove in the edge of the pulley wheel to prevent the drive band slipping off. This should be about 3mm deep and can be either carved out with a sharp knife, sawn out with a tenon saw or filed out with a small file.

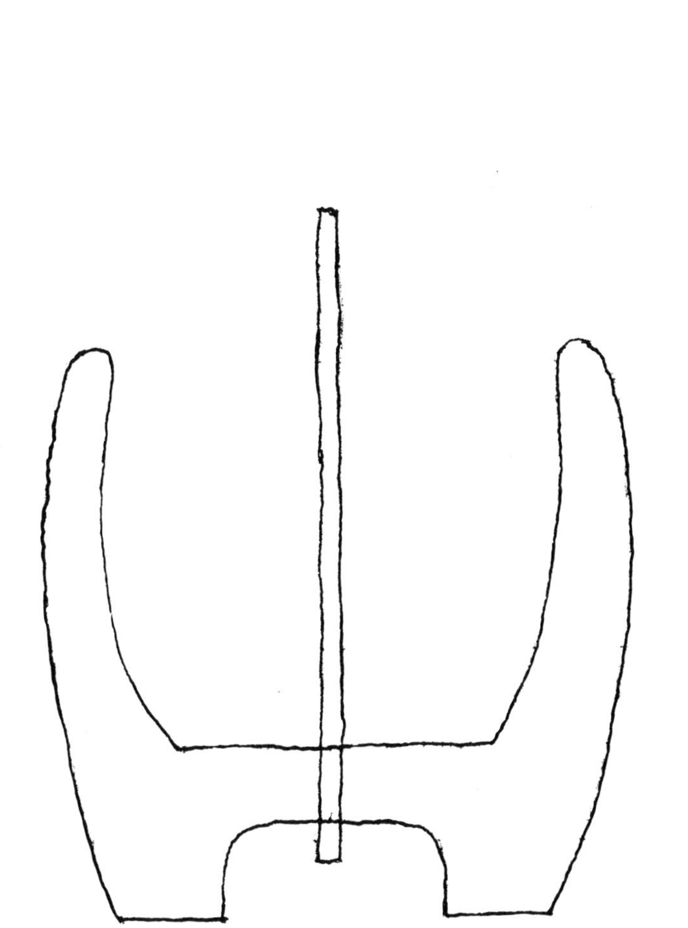

Figure 17b. Side view of flyer showing hole in centre.

Figure 17a. Scale drawing (half actual size) of flyer.

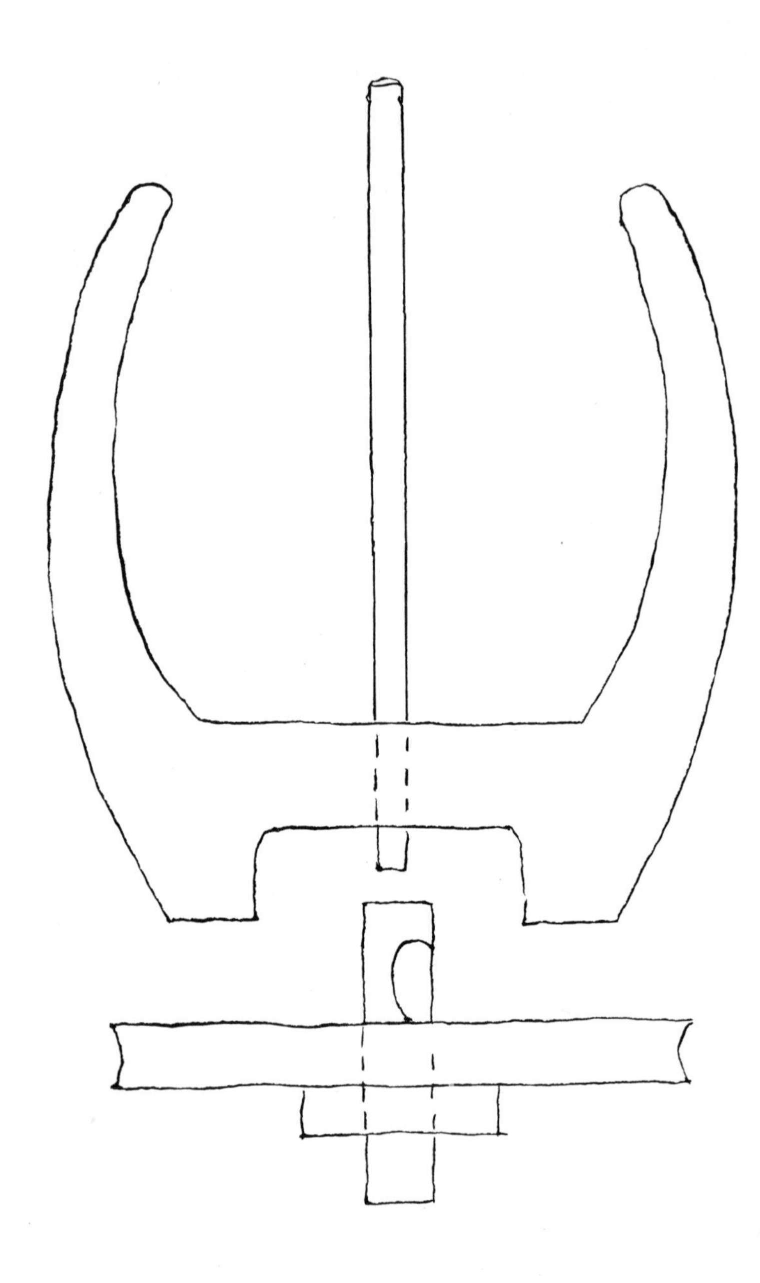

Figure 18. Lining up the pulley wheel and flyer.

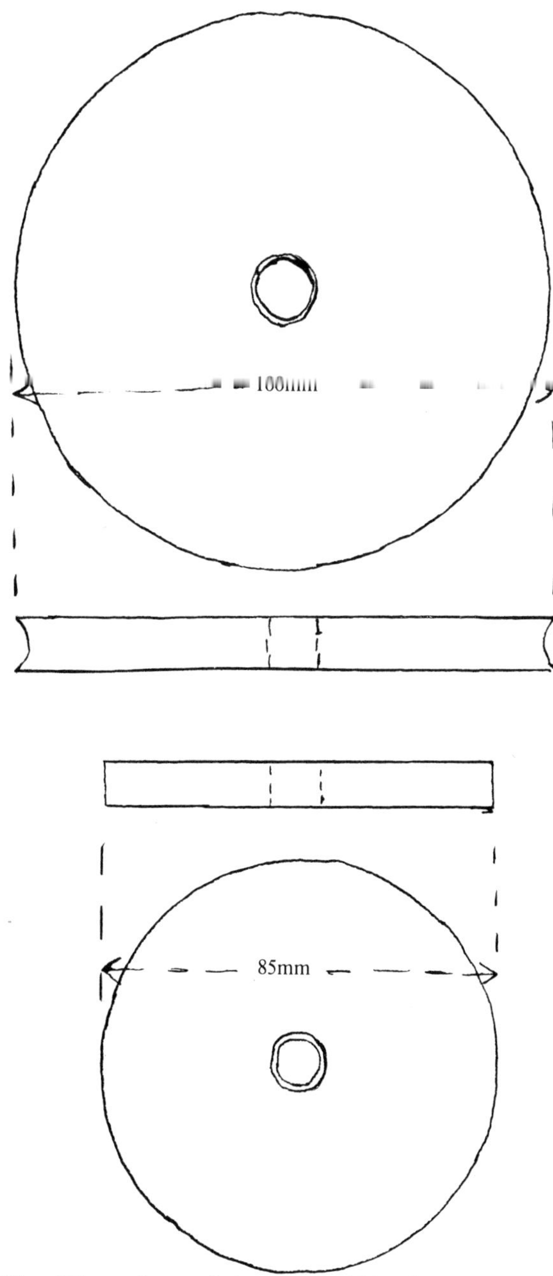

Figure 19. Dimensions of the two bobbin flanges (front and side view).

The Bobbin

The final piece to make is the bobbin (see Figure 19). The two flanges are cut from 9mm ply. One is 85mm in diameter, the other 100mm. A groove similar to the one in the pulley wheel should be made in the edge of the larger one. Once again what you use for the shaft of the bobbin will depend on what you can get. The ideal material is wooden dowel with a 7mm hole drilled through it from end to end. The piece should be 110mm long. This, however, may be hard to find and difficult to make. You might find a suitable piece of bamboo sold in D.I.Y. or garden shops. Metal pipe will do but wood runs better. Whatever you use, drill the centre of the two ends to take it. Slide them onto the shaft, and glue them, leaving 3mm of shaft protruding at each end as in Figure 20.

When the bobbin is set hard it can be slipped onto the spindle of the flyer, small end first, where it should rotate freely. If it does not, check whether the bobbin sides are rubbing against the flyer or if the bobbin is binding on the spindle. In either case, sand or file down the offending piece until the bobbin runs free.

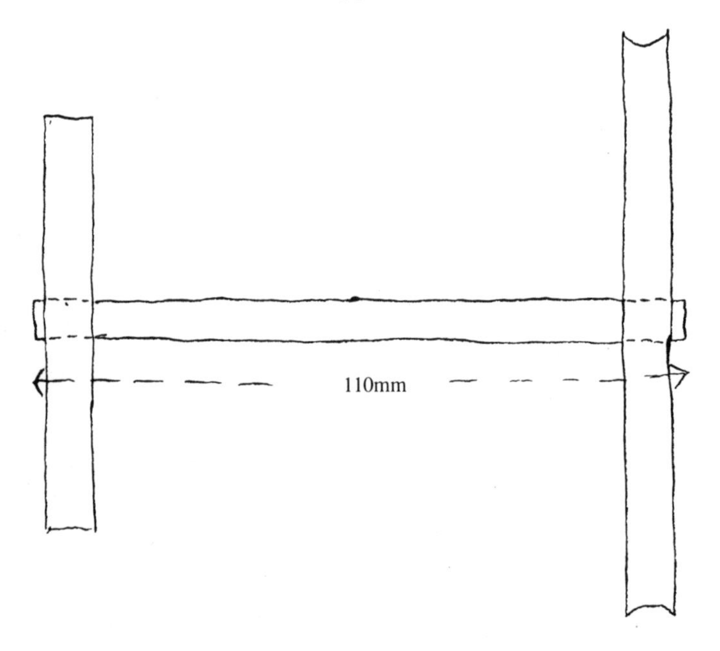

Figure 20. The bobbin flanges attached to the shaft showing protrusion at each end.

Sand and varnish the bobbin and flyer. When they are dry replace the bobbin on the spindle and fit the assembly into the base, holding it in place with the second side piece. Check that the flyer assembly can rotate smoothly and then glue and pin the second side of the base into position. When the glue is dry, sand and varnish the base and your spinner is almost constructed.

Final Additions

Two small additions should be made before connecting the spinner to the treadle. A brake is to be fitted to the bobbin and hooks must be added to the flyer arms. The brake consists of a length of nylon fishing line fastened at one end to a spring (Figure 12) and at the other end to a peg set in the base (Figure 14) which can be turned to tighten or loosen the brake on the bobbin. The peg can be made of a 60mm length of 6mm wooden dowel with a large wooden bead glued to one end to make a knob. This peg, to which the nylon brake cord is attached, is inserted in a 6mm hole drilled in the end of the base strengthener (Figure 14).

The last additions are ten small steel or brass cuphooks which have to be fixed to the arms of the flyer, five in each. They should be placed every 12mm along the arms, one set starting 10mm from the end of one arm, the other set starting 8mm from the end of the other arm. Note that in Figure 12 one set of cuphooks are hidden from view.

Place your spinner on the sewing machine base. You will see that there are two holes in the base through which the drive belt from the treadle passes. If your base is minus a belt or if it has perished or broken you will be able to obtain a replacement from a sewing machine shop. The old belts were leather, more modern ones are rubber or plastic. Connect up the belt, shortening it if necessary and position the spinner so that the belt runs over the drive pulley resting in the groove. Connect the spinner to the base with two 40mm hinges (see Figure 12). You will have to place a small piece of ply 40mm × 20mm × 12mm under the hinges attached to the base in order that they lie flat. You can now treadle and your spinner will turn. If the belt is too slack you can slip a wedge under the back of the base to tighten it. If there is still too much slack you will have to shorten the belt but do not do so if it is possible to take up the slack with wedges. Belts will tighten and slacken according to temperature and humidity so it is best to keep your options open.

Using the Spinner

Having already learnt to use a spindle and a Great Wheel you will have little difficulty understanding the theory of your new spinner. Getting the hang of using it will take a little longer so be prepared to be humbled by what seems a ludicrously easy task.

First tie a leader about a metre long onto the bobbin of the spinner. Thread it around one of the hooks and then with a wire threader (see Figure 21) pull it through the centre of the pulley wheel pipe and out of the orifice as shown in Figure 12. Hold onto this leader with your left hand, treadle with your feet, and with the right hand adjust the bobbin brake until you feel the leader being pulled into the spinner. You will notice that the leader is being twisted and wound onto the storage bobbin at the same time. This is the key to continuous spinning. Take a rolag of carded wool, similar to that prepared for spinning on the Great Wheel, in your right hand and lay the end of the leader into the rolag as you did when joining on with your previous spinners. Allow some twist to slip past your left hand fingers and to run up the leader into the rolag. At the same time thin out the rolag to the thickness of yarn you require by moving your right hand away from the spinner. This thinning out of the rolag is called draughting.

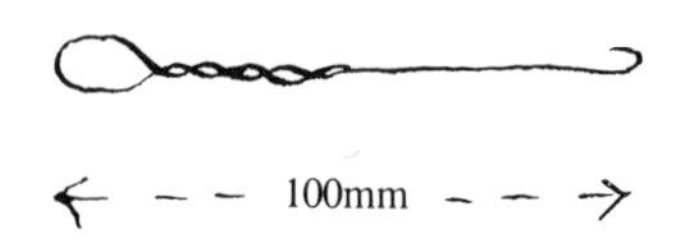

Figure 21. Wire threader for attaching leader.

Three things are happening at once. You are twisting the thread by treadling, you are controlling the flow of that twist onto the rolag by the loosening or tightening of your grip on the thread with your left hand and you are draughting out the fibres with your right hand. The combination of concurrent draughting and twisting is what makes a thread and when they are in the right proportions to each other they make a thread which is surprisingly strong. During this twisting and draughting you will have resisted the wheel's tendency to wind your thread onto the bobbin but as soon as you have a length of thread between your hands stop fighting it and allow the bobbin to pull the thread onto itself moving your hands towards the orifice as you do so. When you have about 20cm of thread left between your left hand and the orifice stop the flow of thread onto the bobbin and start again.

Spinning is not a difficult skill to learn but it is a difficult skill to communicate. The opportunity to watch a spinner followed by lots of practice is the key to success. Stick to it and suddenly you will find it is second nature. Do not be taken in by the myth that spinning is a mysterious and complicated art requiring years of practice and lots of expensive tuition. This just is not true. As I have said before, it is just a knack, no more difficult than riding a bicycle and you will pick it up just as quickly.

5
BUILDING A SPINNING WHEEL

Before starting to build your own spinning wheel go to your local library and get a book on the subject (see *Further Reading*). If you have not looked carefully at wheels before you will be struck by two things—firstly, the variety of design and, secondly, how complicated they look. Wheels of course were not just decorative pieces of furniture to stand in a corner; they were an essential and much used tool of everyday life and so a lot of time and thought went into their making and their design. Wheels had to be convenient and comfortable to use and each spinners idea of what was convenient and comfortable might vary from that of his neighbour. They also were built to last and so they were put together with precision and careful craftsmanship. The large number of old wheels still in use today are proof of the skills of their makers.

For most of us, such skills are beyond our reach and if we are to build our own wheel we must look for some shortcut to compensate for our shortcomings as craftsmen. The wheel I shall describe in this chapter is one answer. Its beauty lies not in its proportions or craftsmanship but in its efficiency and its cheapness. You will not be creating an heirloom but you will make a wheel which will perform as well, if not better, than many of its more elaborate forebears (see Figure 22).

The Materials

A traditional spinning wheel is essentially a simple piece of

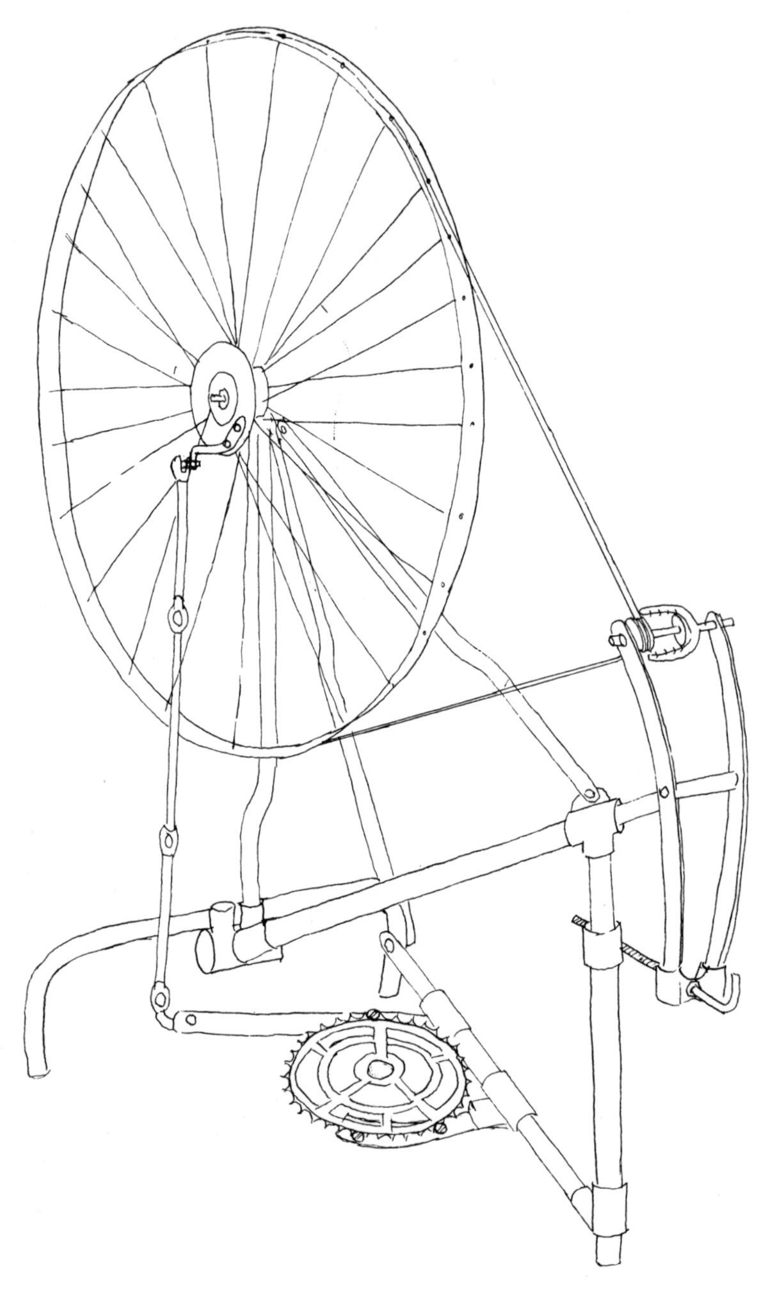

Figure 22. The bicycle spinning wheel.

equipment, a frame which supports a wheel with a foot pedal to turn it, and a flyer connected to the wheel by a drive band. Our spinning wheel will consist of these parts made as simply as possible and with as few refinements or extras as is practical. To make it you will need an old bicycle with at least one sound wheel and an extra pair of handlebars and front forks. Indeed, the instructions provided here assume you are using an old-style bicycle. The best kind of bicycle for the purpose is a heavy old fashioned 'sit up and beg' with a 28-inch or 30-inch wheel. *Avoid dropped handlebars, cable brakes or light-weight racing frames.* If you can find a gem such as an ex-police or ex-post-office bicycle you should feel delighted. They were always made to exacting specifications and built to last. An ex-W.O. bike might also be a possibility. I remember an ex-police bicycle I had when I was young which had been custom built for a particularly tall man and had two crossbars. If only I had it now! Scour the dumps and your neighbour's sheds or barns and see what you can find. Generally speaking, the older the better.

Splitting the Frame

The first thing to do is to dismantle the bicycle you decide to use. If it has been lying out or in a shed for some time it will be rusty and you will need the assistance of penetrating oil to get it apart. Remove the wheels, brakes, pedals, spindle, mud-guards, lights, bell and seat. Everything, in fact, except the front forks and handlebars.

From what is left you are going to construct a metal frame, standing on three legs, to support a wheel and flyer. With a hacksaw split the frame into two parts by cutting through the two metal tubes which connect the front and the back of the bicycle (see Figure 23). Note that the crossbar is cut to leave 300mm attached to the frame (D) and the other tube cut to leave 300mm attached to the front forks. Set aside the front forks and handlebars. They will be used later to make a foot pedal. Next, remove the two pieces of tubing which make up the right hand side of the rear wheel support. The one which runs from under the seat to the rear wheel hub can be unbolted; the other which runs from the rear wheel hub to the pedal hub must be hack-sawed off as close to the hub as possible.

You are left now with four pieces of metal arranged as in Figure 24. Place the seat support in the vice and make three cuts with a hacksaw on the inside of the upright (see Figure 25a).

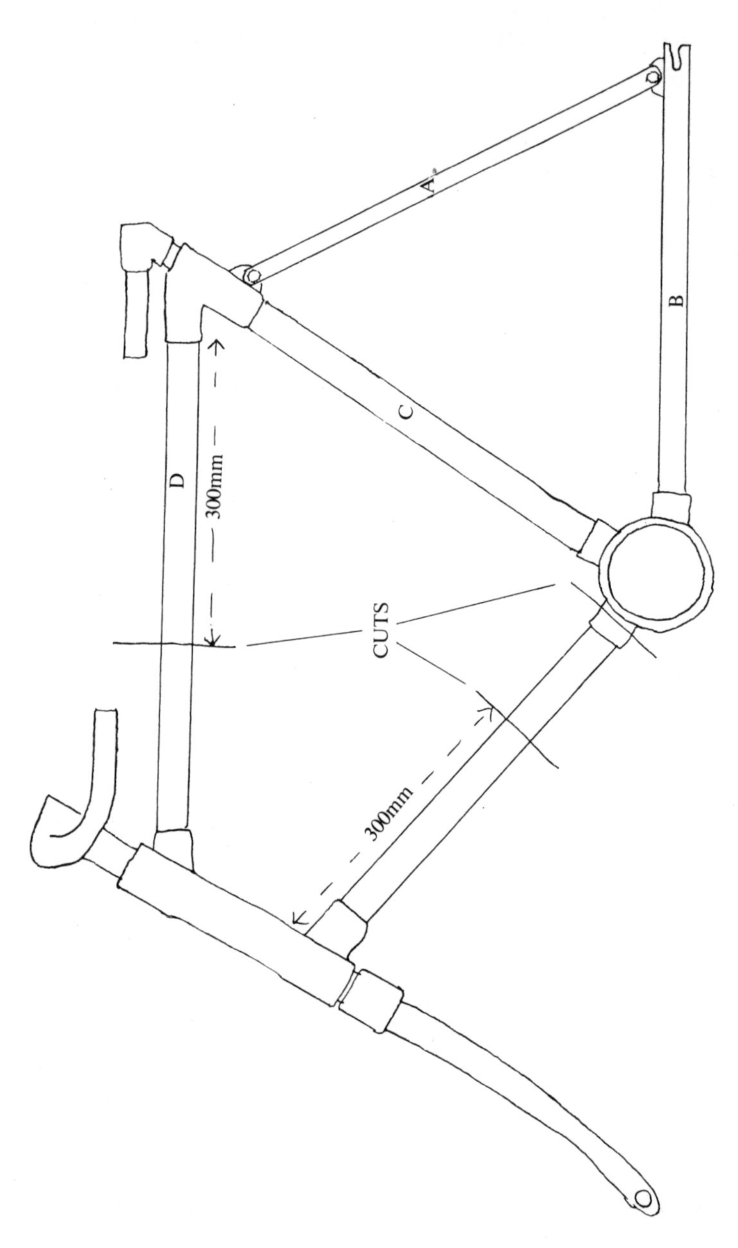

Figure 23. Splitting the frame.

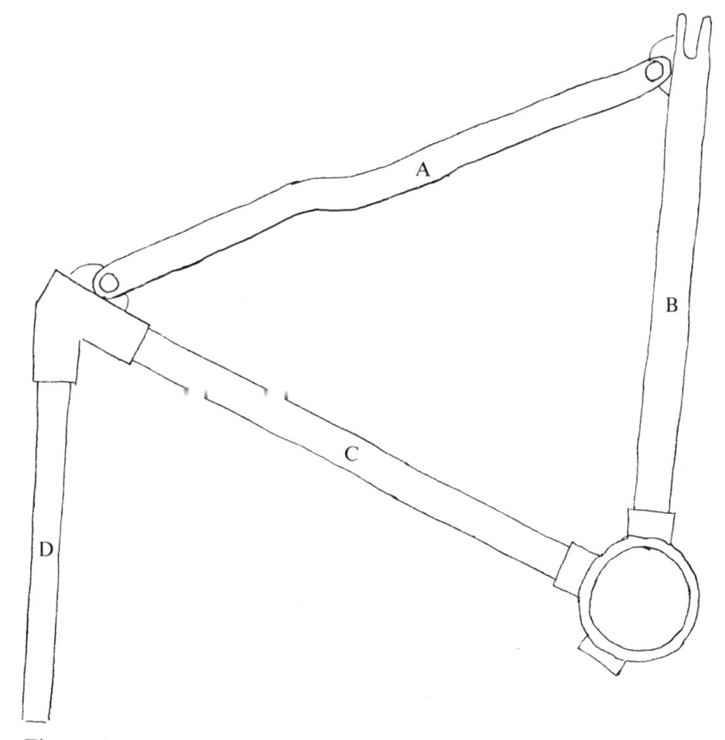

Figure 24. The frame cut to make wheel and flyer support.

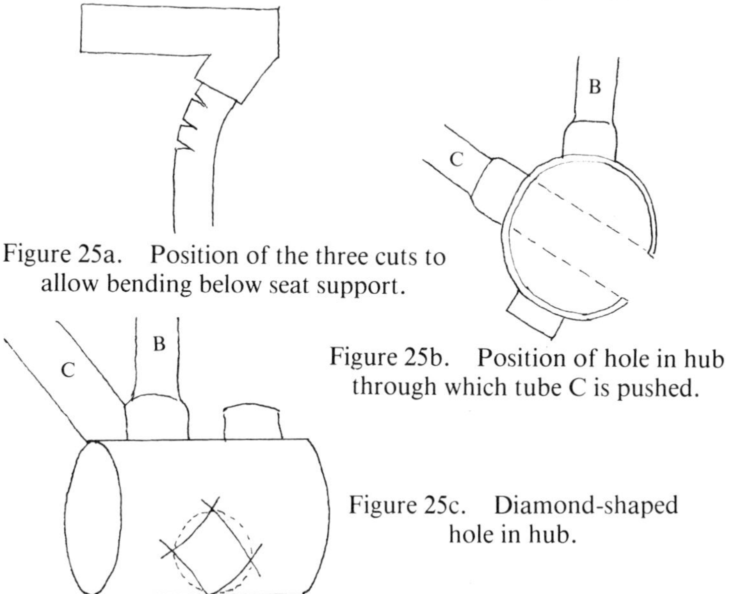

Figure 25a. Position of the three cuts to allow bending below seat support.

Figure 25b. Position of hole in hub through which tube C is pushed.

Figure 25c. Diamond-shaped hole in hub.

Then bend the upright until it is at right angles to the crossbar. The seat support is then re-inserted into its original position in the frame.

Handlebar Legs

Next, the spare handlebars are attached at the base of the hub so as to act as legs. This is done by removing a diamond-shaped piece of metal from the hub so as to allow the handlebar support to be pushed through the hub and up tube C. The diamond-shaped hole therefore must be placed directly opposite tube C. Each side of the diamond-shaped hole should be 25mm in length. These cuts can be made with a hacksaw and the sides then rounded out with a round file (see Figures 25b and 25c). When the handlebar support is entered through this hole you may find that it is not a tight fit. If this is the case place the end of the support in a vice and squeeze it slightly out of shape. You will find that it is then a tight fit in the frame (Figure 26).

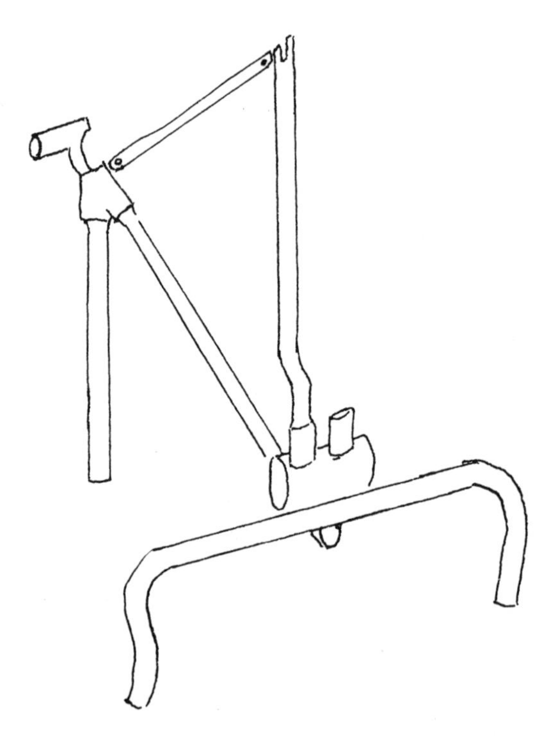

Figure 26. Handlebar legs attached to wheel support frame.

Wheel Support

With the twin to tube A (previously removed from the frame), you now make a supporting stay for the wheel support (see Figure 27). The stay should be attached to tube B 70mm from the top. Drill a 3mm hole through the stay and tube B and fix with a 3mm bolt 20mm long, lock washer and nut. Cut off any excess length of bolt. At the other end, the stay is attached to the handlebars with a 3mm bolt 50mm long. Drill a hole in the stay and handlebars to receive the bolt, fix with a lock washer and nut but in this case, do not cut off the excess length of the bolt.

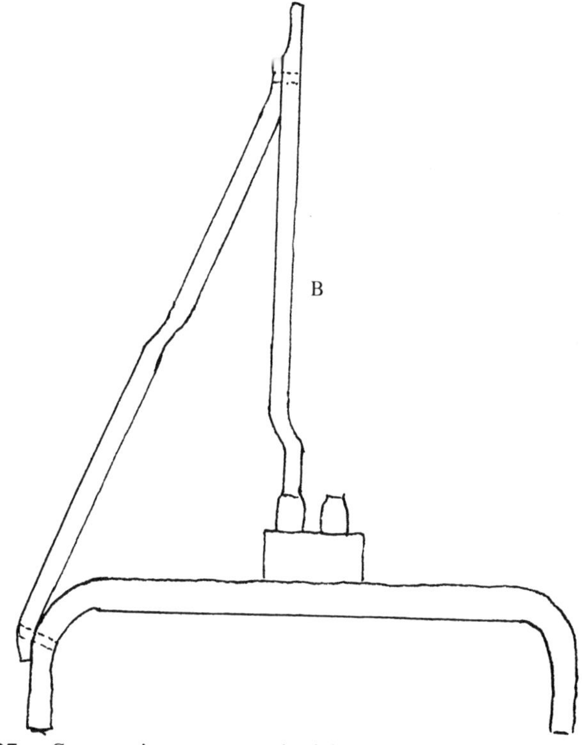

Figure 27. Supporting stay attached from handlebar legs to upright wheel support, tube B.

The Pedal

The next piece to be added is the pedal. This will be made from the front forks and handlebars. First cut off the arms of the handlebars so that the right hand stub of the arms measures 50mm and the left hand one 100mm. Unscrew the locking nut on top of the front forks so that the handlebars are loose in the

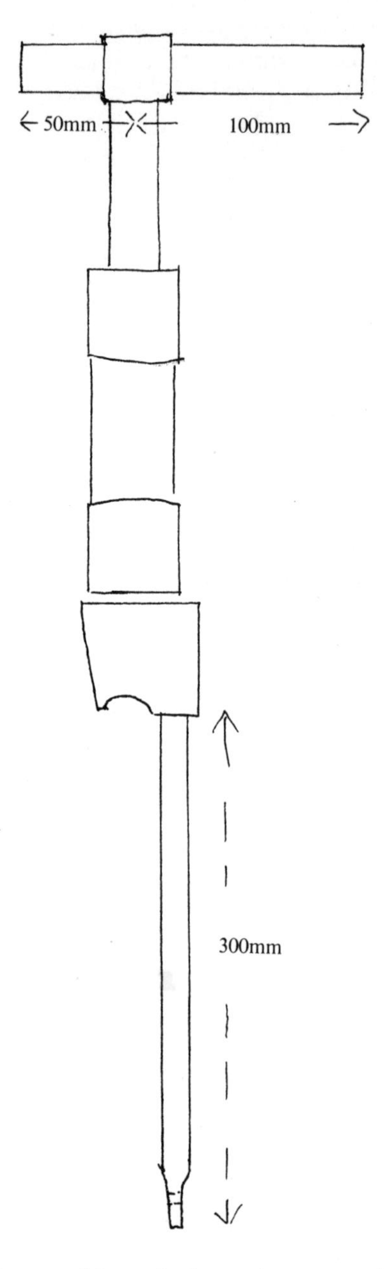

Figure 28. Handlebars and front forks cut in preparation for pedal assembly (front view).

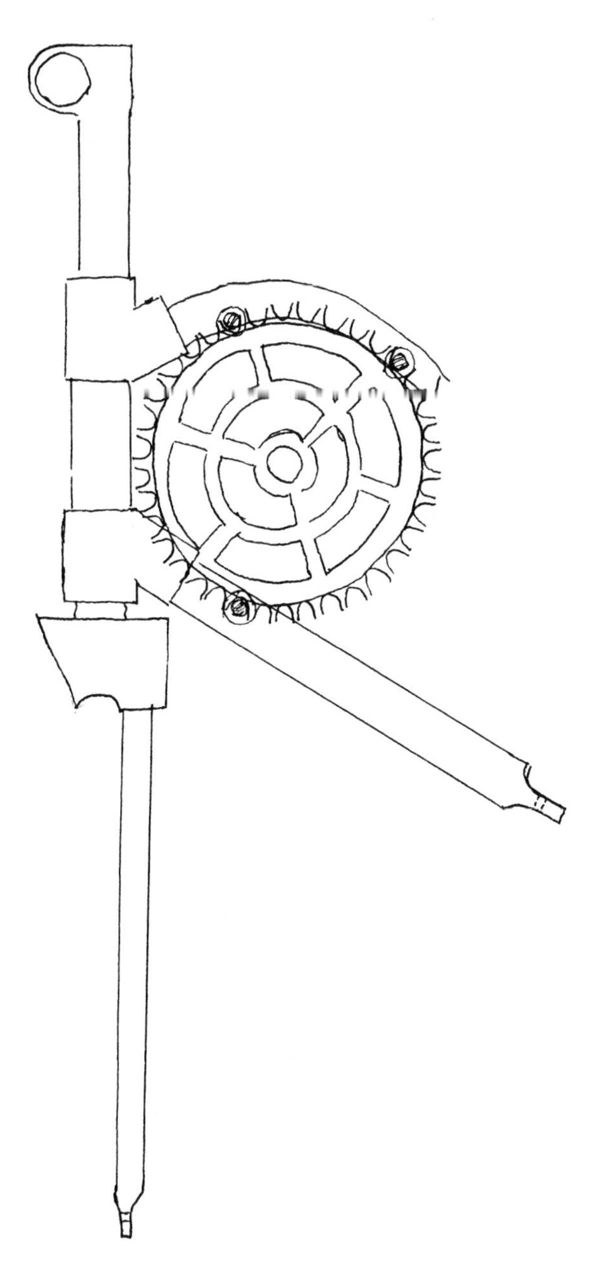

Figure 29. The upper frame tube bent to accommodate the wheel sprocket on the front fork assembly.

front forks. With the hacksaw, cut off the right hand front fork and shorten the left hand one so that it measures 300mm. Flatten the sawn off end in a vice (see Figure 28) and drill a 3mm hole through the centre of the flattened pipe 10mm from its end. Bend the shorter of the frame tubes attached to the front forks so that it will form one of two supporting arms to which the sprocket wheel can be bolted. Free the sprocket wheel from its pedal and bolt it onto the two arms with three 3mm bolts 30mm long, lock washers and nuts as shown in Figure 29.

This assembly is now ready to be attached to the frame. Insert the 100mm arm of the handlebars into the bottom of tube D (see Figure 30) and thread the drilled hole at the other end onto the bolt which holds the supporting strut to the handlebars, fixing it with a lock washer and nut (see Figure 27).

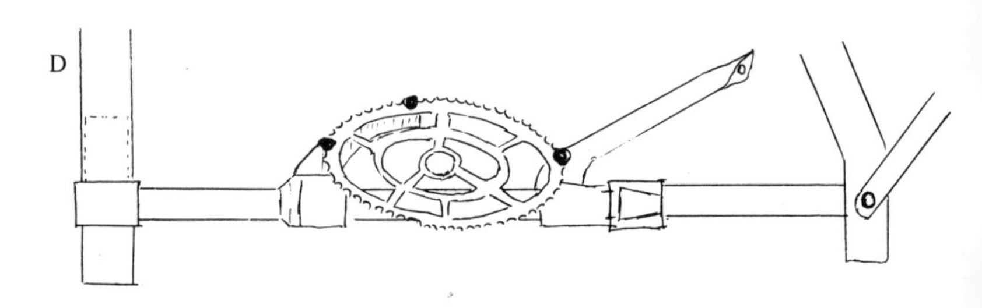

Figure 30. The pedal assembly attached to frame tube D and the handlebars.

Fitting the Wheel

The wheel can now be fitted to the frame. If you have a number of wheels select the one in the best condition, that is, free from rust, not buckled and with all its spokes in place. Remove the old tyre and inner tube if necessary and, if the tape which covers the end of the spokes is worn, replace it with a strong 10mm wide dressmakers tape. Remove the spindle, clean the ball-bearing races, grease and replace ball-bearings, races and locking nuts.

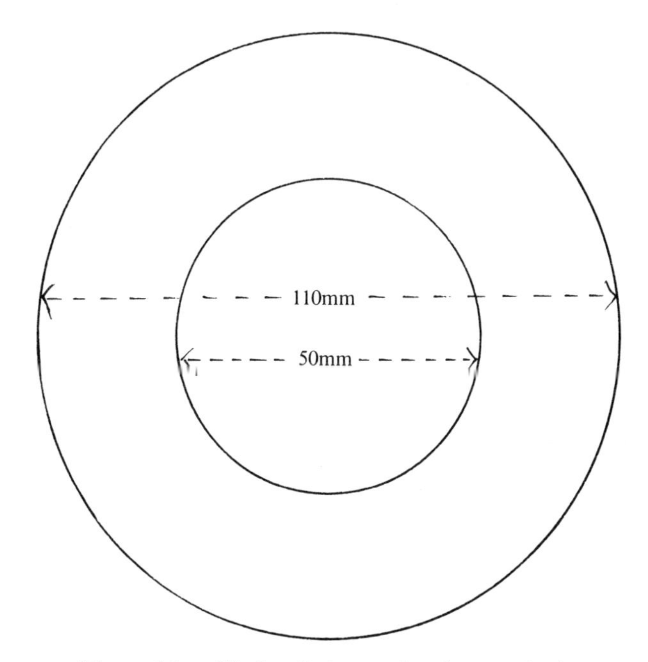

Figure 31. Circle of plywood to be attached to wheel centre.

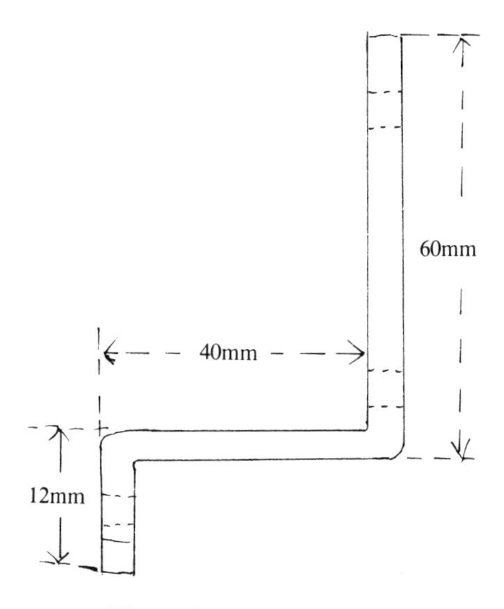

Figure 32. The crank.

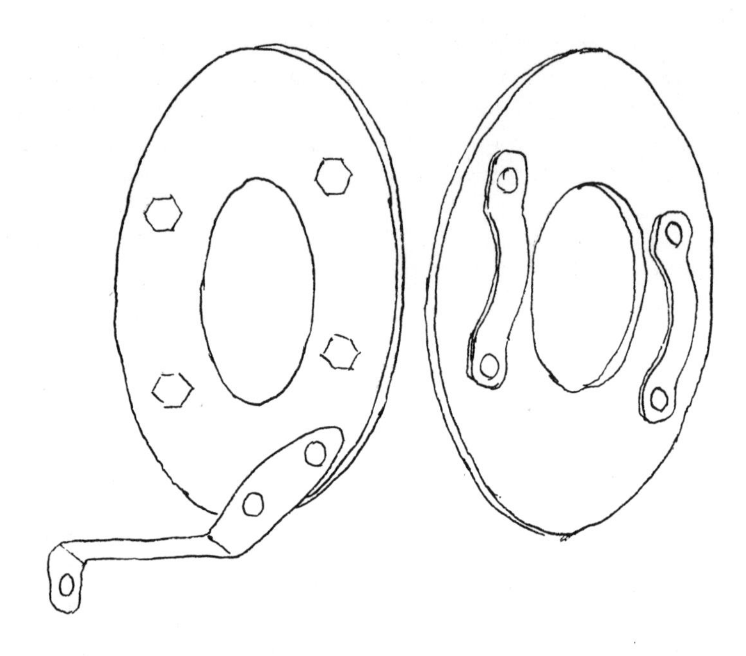

Figure 33. The crank attached to the plywood circle, showing back plates used to attach this to the wheel centre.

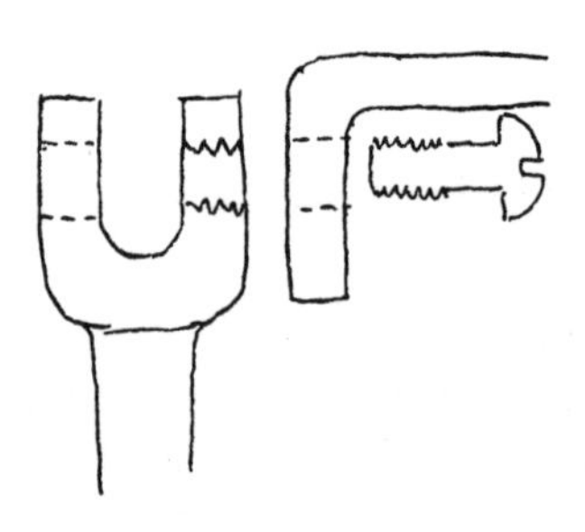

Figure 34. Attaching a front brake link to the crank.

Now cut a circle of 3mm ply, diameter 110mm, with a coping saw and remove a 50mm diameter circle from its centre as shown in Figure 31. From the back brake linkage remove the angled piece of metal which was pivoted just beneath the hub. Bend this piece of metal (as in Figure 32) and attach it to the plywood circle (see Figure 33). Fix the wood circle with its metal attachment to the centre of the wheel with the screws and back plates of the two front brake block guides (see Figure 33). This arrangement provides a handle or crank with which to turn the wheel. Now fix the wheel spindle in its support (tube B) and fix it in a vertical position by tightening the nut on the spindle. The wheel should now revolve smoothly on its bearings.

You will notice that the long arm of the pedal assembly rests on the floor beneath the wheel. This must now be connected to the wheel crank. You will use the two adjustable front brake links and a connecting length of straight wire. Attach one of the links to the wheel crank (Figure 34). To attach the other link to the pedal, first insert the metal angle, originally positioned on the front forks as a brake link, into the flattened end of the long arm of the pedal assembly and fix it with a 5mm bolt, 30mm long, lock washer and nut. Join the second adjustable link to it with the original screw and connect the two links with a 300mm length of brake wire. Adjust the length of the pedal link so that the pedal is held just clear of the floor (see Figure 35).

Figure 35. The pedal link.

The Flyer Assembly

You can now start on the flyer assembly. You will see from Figure 36 that it is made from the extra front forks supported on a rod which passes through the original seat support. The seat support is a 7-shaped piece of metal tubing. With a hacksaw make three cuts in the inside of the upright leg of the '7'. Now bend the two arms so that they are at right angles to each other. The top arm should be 110mm long. If it is too long, cut it to length.

Cut the forks from the tube which joined them to the frame immediately above the fork junction. Bend the two arms apart so that they are 110mm apart at a point 230mm from the extremities of the arms. Cut a 150mm length of brake rod and straighten it if necessary. Drill a hole the same diameter as the brake rod in each arm of the forks 230mm from the ends, to take this rod. Beware of the angle at which these holes must be drilled —parallel to a line across the tops of the forks. Plug each end of the seat support with a 30mm length of dowel and drill similar holes through their centres. The rod can now be inserted through the forks and seat support as a supporting pivot for the forks.

You will notice that the forks are placed asymmetrically on the frame. This is intentional and allows the wheel to line up with the flyer which is to be held by the forks. If your bicycle does not have this 7-shaped seat support, an alternative can be made by using a saddle support tube and saddle support clamp. Pass the supporting rod through the clamp with the two wooden spacers, one on either side of the clamp, threaded on the rod. The spacers should be 2cm and 6cm wide and should hold the forks asymmetrically as in Figure 36. The final addition to the frame is an adjustable screw fitted to the bottom of the forks to allow you to adjust the position of the flyer relative to the wheel.

Cut a 150mm length off the threaded end of the back brake adjusting rod. Bend one end at right angles 30mm from its end. Drill a 5mm hole through the centre of the base of the front forks assembly to take it.

From the store of odd nuts which you accumulated while dismantling the bicycle originally, select one which will slip onto this rod. Slide it to a position 25mm from the bend and fix it in that position by squeezing the nut and rod in a vice. Now slip the adjustable collar which originally fixed the seat to the seat support, onto the upright tube D of the frame and slide it up to a position opposite the adjusting rod. The original back brake adjusting screw with its serrated edge, having first had a segment cut from it (see Figure 37), is placed in the gap in the adjustable collar and the rod is threaded through the collar and screw as in Figure 37. By turning the adjusting rod handle the position of the forks can be altered. Back brake adjusting mechanisms can vary from bicycle to bicycle. The one I used had a threaded rod and nut which controlled the position of the brakes relative to the wheel. If your frame has a different arrangement for

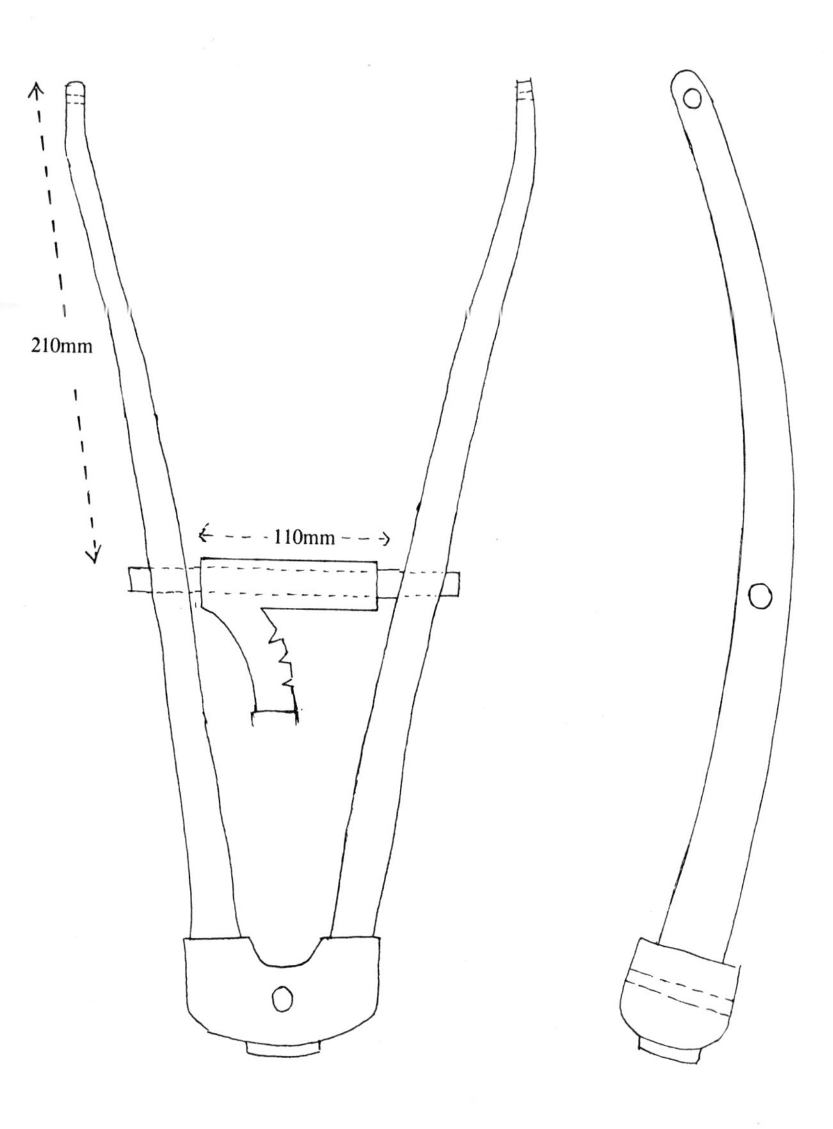

Figure 36. The flyer assembly built from the extra set of front forks.

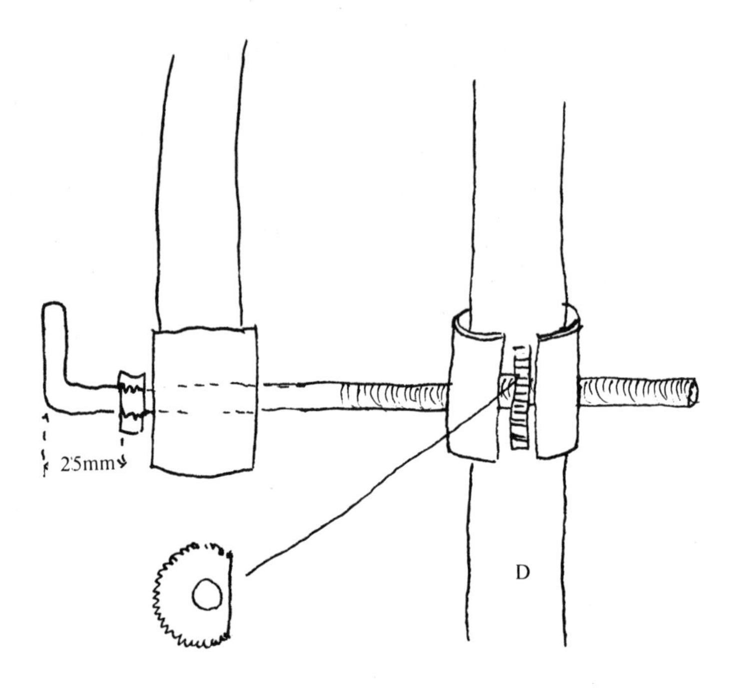

Figure 37. The flyer assembly adjusting rod passing through base of front forks and the collar on frame tube D.

adjusting the brakes, then buy a 15cm threaded bolt, 5cm in diameter, and nut and use them in the same way.

Making the Spinner

The last and perhaps the trickiest piece of the wheel to make is the spinner assembly which is to be supported in two leather bearings on top of the forks. This spinner has some similarities to the Indian Head Spinner but differs in one essential element. Whereas the Indian Head Spinner has a single drive band which drives the flyer round and an adjustable brake which controls the bobbin, this spinner has a double drive band from the wheel, one strand of which drives the flyer and the other the bobbin. The spinner is comprised of three parts: one a U-shaped flyer attached to a spindle; a bobbin; and a pulley wheel which drives the spindle. I suggest you make them in that order.

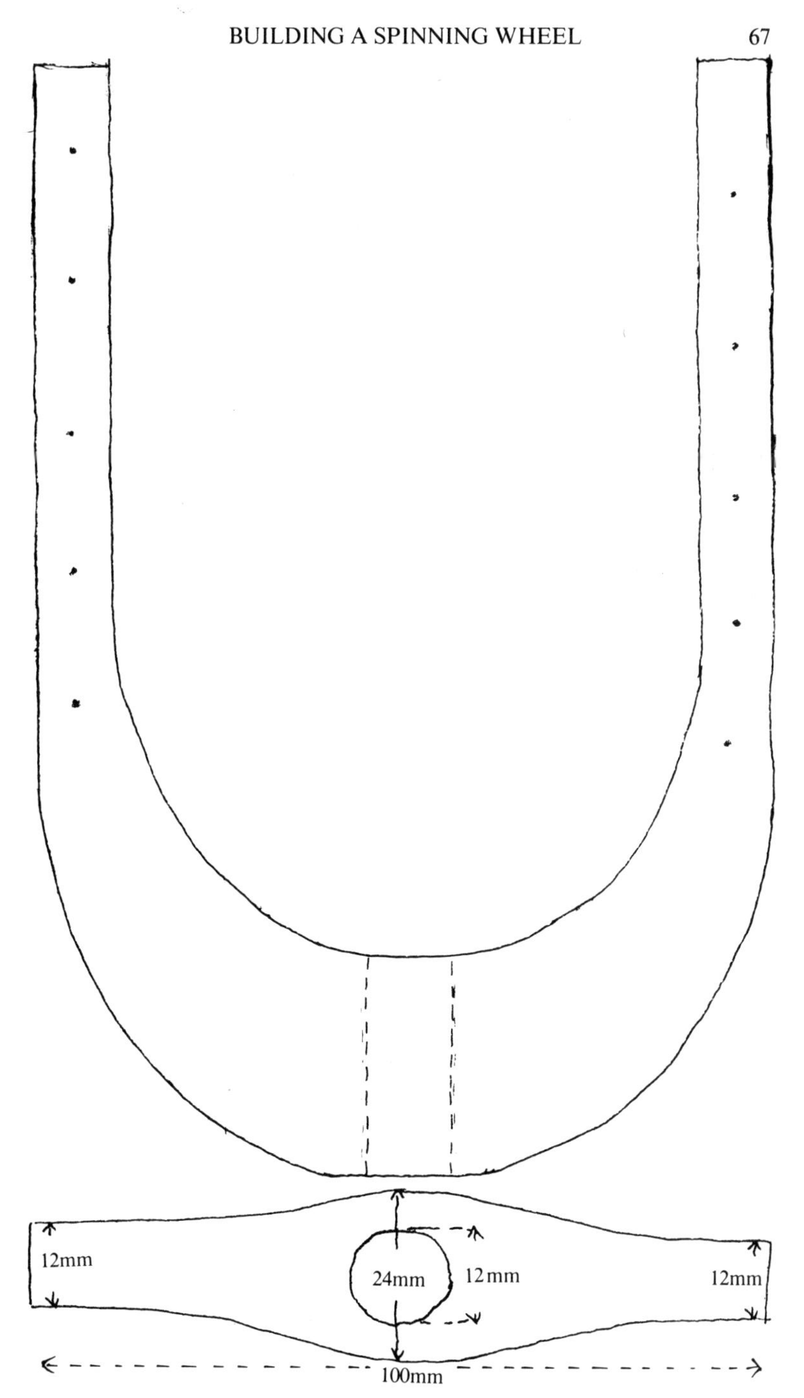

Figure 38. Pattern (actual size) of the flyer.

The Flyer

The U-shaped flyer is made of two pieces of 12mm plywood glued together. Cut two pieces of ply 150mm × 120mm, glue them together and let them set in a vice. Trace the shape of the flyer onto the wood and cut it out with a coping saw. The drawing is actual size. With a surform, shape the arms down to the measurements shown in Figure 38. Drill a 12mm hole through the centre of the flyer to take the metal spindle.

The Spindle

The spindle is comprised of two parts: a 100mm length of steel tube, outside diameter 12mm, inside diameter 9mm; and a 220mm length of 10mm diameter steel rod. First take the length of tube and with a round file make a 9mm hole in it, centred 20mm from one end (Figure 39). Find a washer which fits tightly onto the tube. File it down so that it is 15mm approx. in diameter and fix it with Araldite 13mm from this same end (Figure 39). File 55mm of the steel rod down to 9mm diameter so that it can be pushed into the tube leaving 170mm protruding. Before fixing it in this position some further shaping must be done to the other end. The rod must be filed down in two steps, the first step a 7mm square section 30mm long, and the second step, a round section of 7mm diameter, 25mm long (Figure 39). Coat the inside of tube with Araldite and slide the rod into it leaving

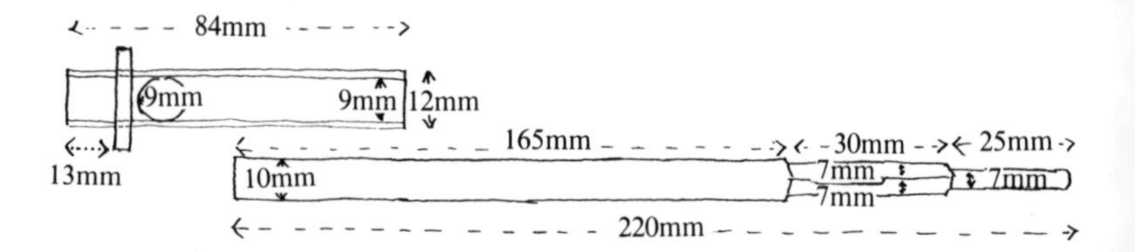

Figure 39. Diagram of the spindle rod and tube.

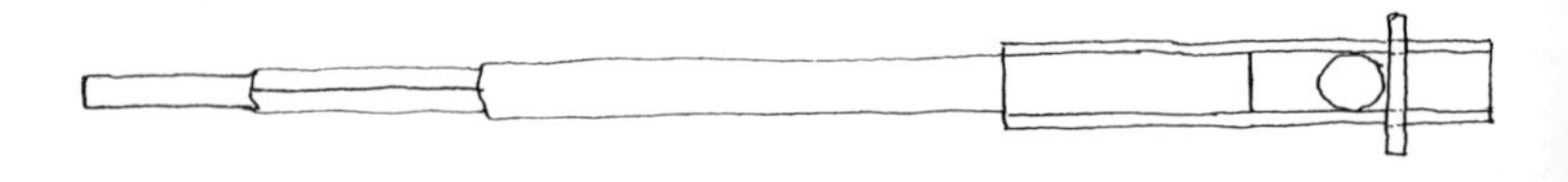

Figure 40. The completed spindle.

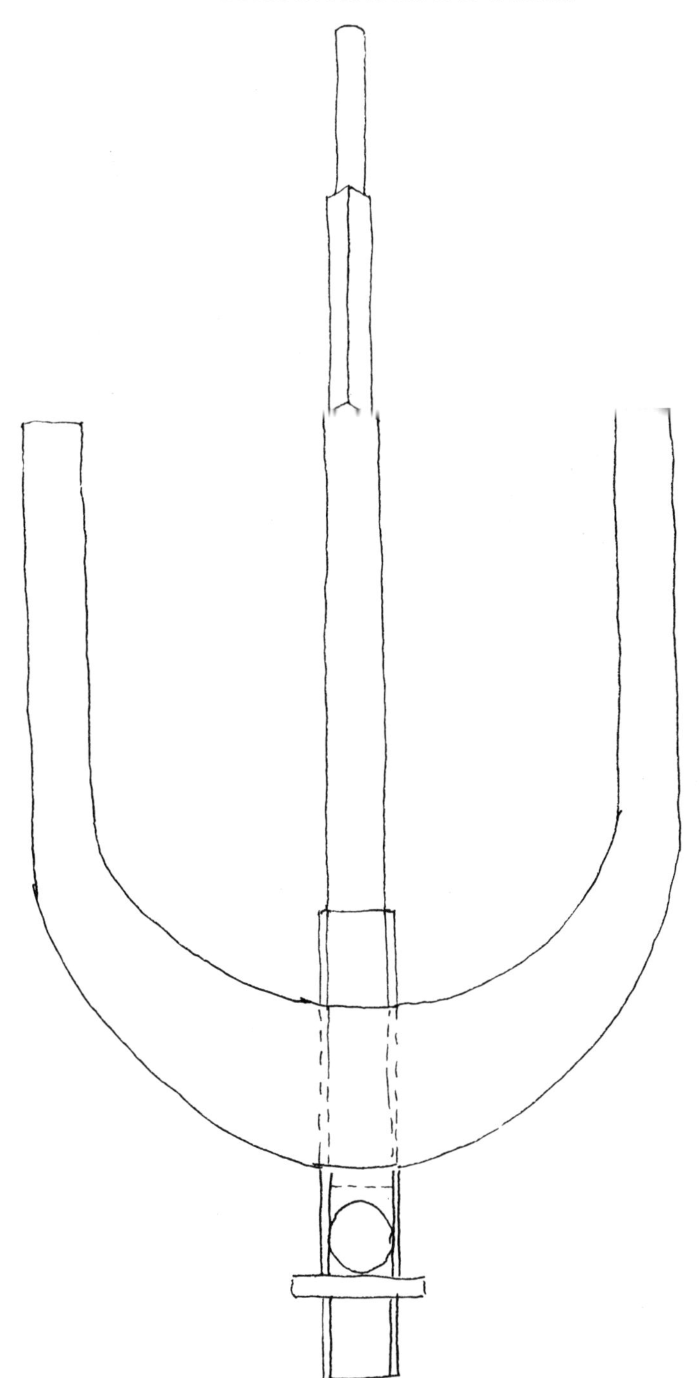

Figure 41. The spindle in position in the flyer.

170mm protruding (Figure 40). Leave to set. When it has set slide the spindle into the U-shaped flyer (Figure 41) positioning it so that the end with the washer and hole in it protrudes 40mm from the flyer. Note the position, slide the flyer off the spindle, apply Araldite to the inside of the flyer and replace the spindle. Note that the hole in the spindle must be positioned as in Figure 41. Screw five small cuphooks into each arm of the flyer in the positions marked in Figure 38.

The Bobbin

The bobbin is similar to that made for the Indian Head Spinner in the last chapter. It has two flanges attached to a spindle; one, a 55mm diameter circle of 9mm plywood, and the other is made up of two circles of 9mm plywood glued together. One circle is 70mm diameter, the other 50mm diameter. A groove 5mm deep

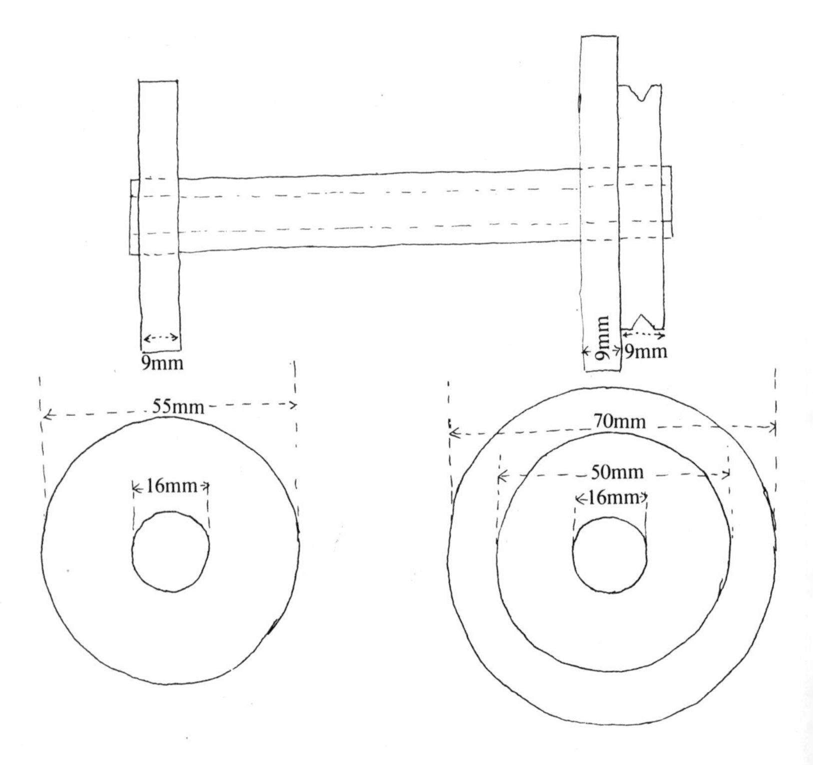

Figure 42. The bobbin and bobbin pulley, showing the protrusion of the shaft.

is cut around the edge of the smaller circle. The flanges are fixed on a 115mm length of wooden tube such as bamboo with an outside diameter of 16mm and an inside diameter of 12mm. Drill a hole the same size as the outside diameter of the tube in both flanges and slide them onto the tube, fixing them in position with glue. Leave 3mm of tube protruding from each flange (Figure 42). It is well worth having at least three bobbins for each wheel. This prevents you having to wind the bobbin clear each time it is filled—an empty one can be substituted instead. It also allows you to fill two bobbins, set them in a stand and then ply them onto a third bobbin to make a two-ply yarn. There will be more about plying later.

The Drive Pulley

The last component to make is the drive pulley (see Figure 43). This is made from two 60mm circles of 12mm ply glued together. Two grooves about 3mm and 6mm deep are cut in the outside edge of the pulley using either a file, a saw or a sharp knife. Drill a 7mm hole through the centre of the pulley. With a small triangular file enlarge it to a 7mm square, for this pulley is intended to sit on the square section of the spindle. Cut two 25mm square brass or steel plates. Drill and file a 7mm square

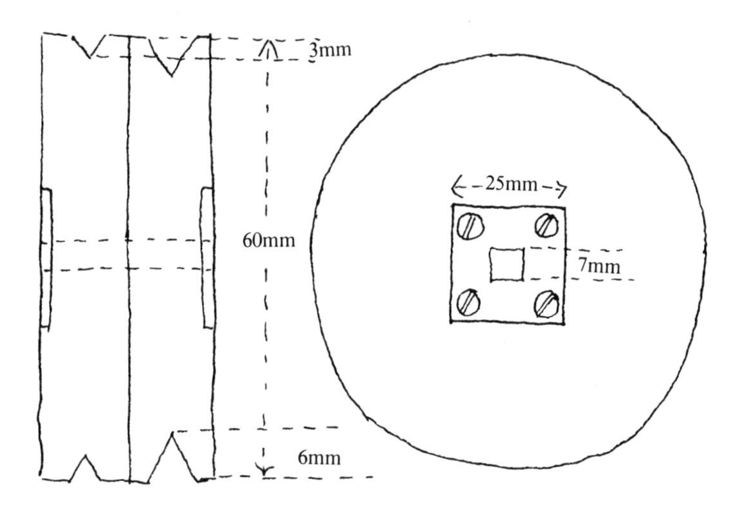

Figure 43. The drive pulley.

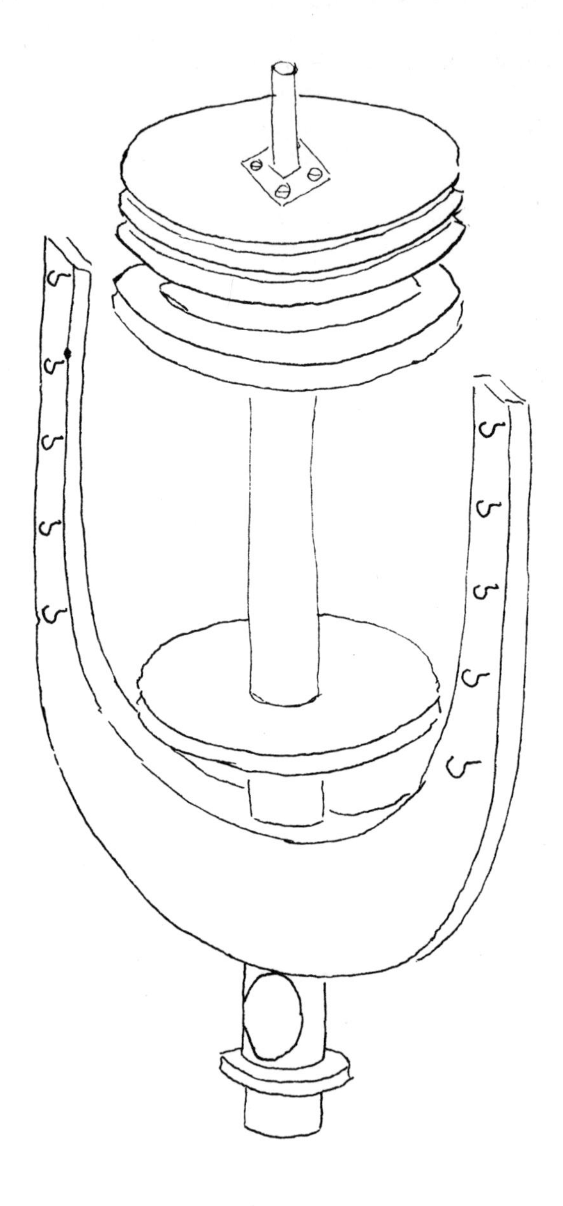

Figure 44. The completed spinner, showing the spindle, the bobbin, the bobbin pulley, the drive pulley and the flyer.

out of the centre of each plate. Drill and counter-sink 3mm holes in each corner of the plates. Chisel out a 25mm square on each side of the pulley and screw the two plates into them. Take care to line the squares up with each other on either side of the pulley, which will now slide snugly onto the square section of the spindle.

The Supports

The assembly, flyer, bobbin and pulley are now ready to be fitted to the forks. A thick leather support, 40mm × 20mm is fixed with a 3mm nut and bolt 20mm long and washers to each arm of the forks. Viewed from above the wheel, the right hand support, should have a 12mm hole made in it—the left hand support, an 8mm hole. The spindle is then suspended between these two tough leather supports which should bend just enough to slip the spindle between them.

The wheel is connected to the flyer by a strong plied linen or cotton cord. It is one large loop with the ends glued together and folded double. One loop goes around the drive pulley, the other around the bobbin pulley. Because the diameter of the bobbin pulley is smaller than the diameter of the drive pulley, the bobbin will rotate faster than the flyer. This difference in rotating speed is what causes the thread to wind on while spinning. The adjusting rod fitted at the bottom of the forks can now be used to tighten or loosen the drive band.

Using Your Spinning Wheel

Spinning on this wheel is much the same as on the Indian Head Spinner. It will, however, take you some time to get used to the treadling. You may find you want to fix a small lead weight to the inside of the wheel rim at a point which counter-balances the weight of the pedal. This will tend to make pedalling a smoother, more consistent operation. Once you can treadle without having to concentrate on it, tie a leader onto the flyer as described in the previous chapter, card up some wool and give it a spin. Experiment with the drive band adjusting rod until you find the wheel taking in the spun thread as it suits you. Tighten the band for quicker take-up, loosen it for a slower, weaker, take-up. Remember that, as with previous spinners, practice, practice and more practice is the key to success.

You may wish to ply your thread into a two-ply yarn. To do this place two full bobbins in a holder which allows them to rotate freely. Tie the two threads onto a leader and feed them into the flyer as you treadle. By adjusting the tension of the drive band you can adjust the speed at which the threads are drawn onto the bobbin. This will vary the amount of twist that is put into them. The two threads can be tightly or loosely twisted around each other. Note that most yarns are plied together with a twist opposing the twist of each single thread. So if you spin your single thread 'Z' twist, ply it up 'S' twist. That means pedalling the wheel in the opposite direction to that used for spinning single.

6
THE TABLE LOOM

Cloth is the result of interlacing two sets of threads; one set stretched lengthwise down the cloth, the other set stretched across it. Weaving is the method of making cloth, the system for interlacing these two sets of threads. In its simplest forms weaving can produce rectangles of cloth ranging in size from a place mat to a bolt of cloth.

For those who are interested in producing textured, patterned or shaped cloth there are many books and a few are listed at the back of this book (see *Useful Information*).

In this book I am sticking to basics, to learning how to produce plain cloth on looms that you can make yourself. Once you have grasped the basics you can proceed to greater things if and when you wish. How you approach the business of making things is a matter of personal preference. Some will just want to follow their nose and see how things turn out. Others may want to do some reading first. There are some interesting books on colour and design in textiles.

Plain Weave

Anyone can weave and most people have done so already. If you have ever darned a hole in a sock you have woven! If you have been deprived of this enriching experience find a sock with a hole in it and darn it. The system is pretty straightforward. First a thread is stretched back and forth from top to bottom of the hole until the hole is covered with a series of parallel threads.

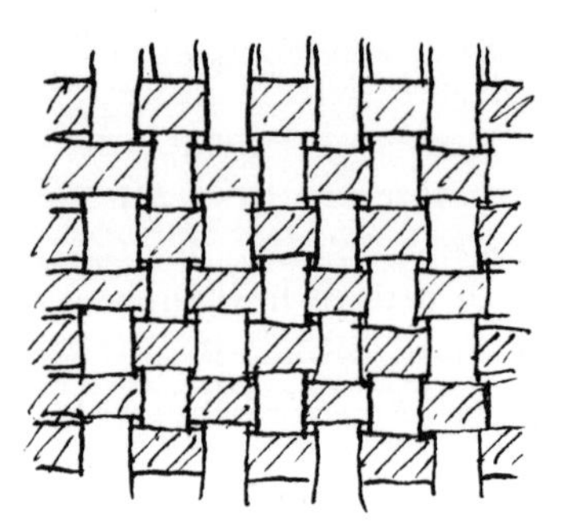

Figure 45. Plain weave.

Then a second series of threads is stretched from side to side, this set interlacing with the first set. Each thread goes alternately over and under the threads it crosses. Now, I know you probably know all this already but the explanation is included because what your darning has produced is *plain weave* (see Figure 45). For some reason it also gets called 'tabby'! Tabby is a perfectly good description of a cat, but not of weaving, and most people will want to stick to calling it plain weave. The strongest cloths are usually made of plain weave. Canvas and thornproof tweed are two examples.

Twill

There is one other basic weave which I will mention—*twill.* The basis is the same two sets of interlaced threads, but instead of each thread going alternatively over and under every thread which it crosses, each thread goes over two and under two of the

Figure 46. Twill.

threads which it crosses and does so in a progressive way (as in Figure 46). It is recognized by the diagonal lines which appear on the surface of the cloth. It is the traditional weave for tweed and blankets and it produces a more flexible cloth than plain weave. So back to the darning mushroom for exercise number two. Find another sock with a hole in it and darn it using twill. First darn in the vertical threads as in the first exercise. Then, using Figure 47 as a guide, start at the top right hand corner and darn over and under the vertical threads according to the following sequence:

Line A Over 1, 2. Under 3, 4. Over 5, 6.
Line B Under 6. Over 5, 4. Under 3, 2. Over 1.
Line C Under 1, 2. Over 3, 4. Under 5, 6.
Line D Over 6. Under 5, 4. Over 3, 2. Under 1.

Start again at Line A and repeat the sequence.

As with all weaving, talking or writing about it just makes it sound more complicated than it is, so try it and then read the previous paragraph again just to be sure that you have it right. If you have, you know what plain weave and twill are and you can call yourself a weaver! But here you hit a snag. You will find that

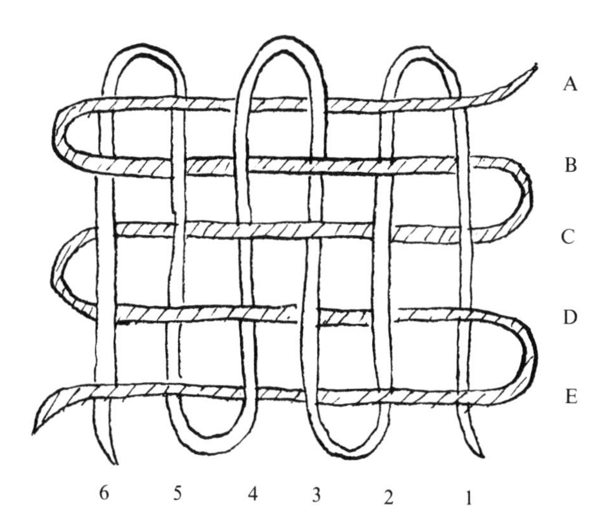

Figure 47. Diagram of twill weave.

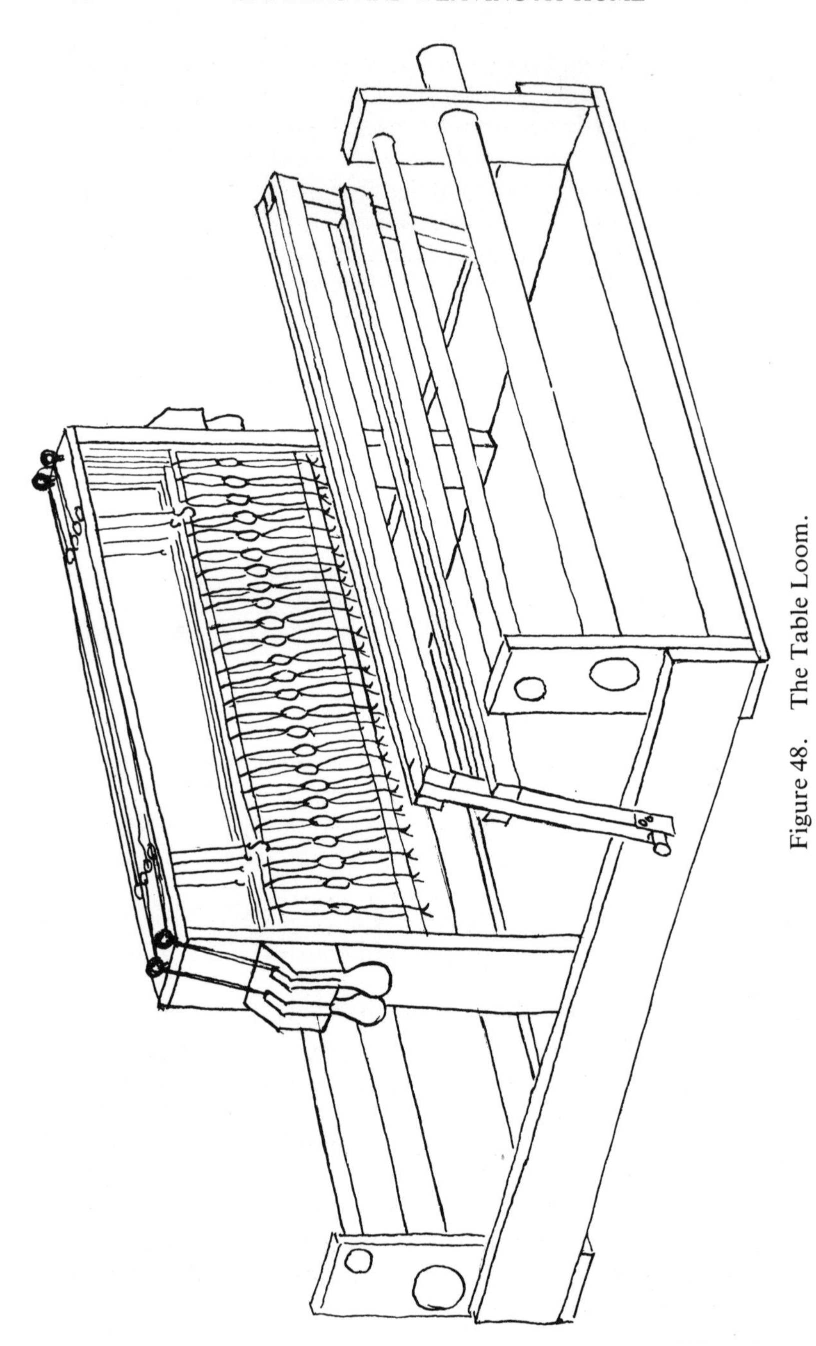

Figure 48. The Table Loom.

you are limited by the socks with holes in them that you can beg, borrow, or wear out. The answer to your problem is the loom.

BUILDING A TABLE LOOM

In this chapter you will find plans and instructions for building a loom on which you will be able to weave cloth up to approximately 50cm wide. In the next chapter there will be plans and instructions for building a larger loom on which it will be possible to weave cloth up to a metre wide.

Before starting to build either loom try and find a loom to look at and preferably see it in use. Exhibitors at local craft fairs or local weavers are usually glad to be of help to anyone with a genuine interest. This will give you an idea of what functions the various parts of the loom perform, and a few minutes observation will be worth more than a thousand words. Although there may be many minor variations between the loom you may see and the one described here, all looms are basically the same and the time spent locating a loom to look at will be amply rewarded.

The Sides

So to work. Firstly, I will describe the construction of a loom designed to stand on the table and to produce cloth up to 50cm wide. Metric measurements are used throughout. Buy finished wood, that is, timber which has already been planed smooth, and ask for well-dried wood. It is less likely to twist out of square later on. Ask a timber merchant or a D.I.Y. shop for advice about the type of wood to use. One of the softer hardwoods—pine or birch—would be ideal. Study Figure 49. You can make up the two side frames; first, the left side frame, as in Figure 56 and then the right side frame, a mirror image of it. The base piece is 72cm × 10cm × 2cm. The two end uprights are 26cm × 10cm × 2cm and the centrally placed upright is 49cm × 10cm × 2cm. Drill the end uprights to take the front and back rollers and front and back beams (Figure 51) and screw and glue them to the base piece. Now add the lift blocks (Figure 52) and the shaft guides (Figure 53) to the central upright (Figure 54) and screw and glue this upright to the base. Next make the second side frame to the same measurements but a mirror image of the first, as mentioned earlier.

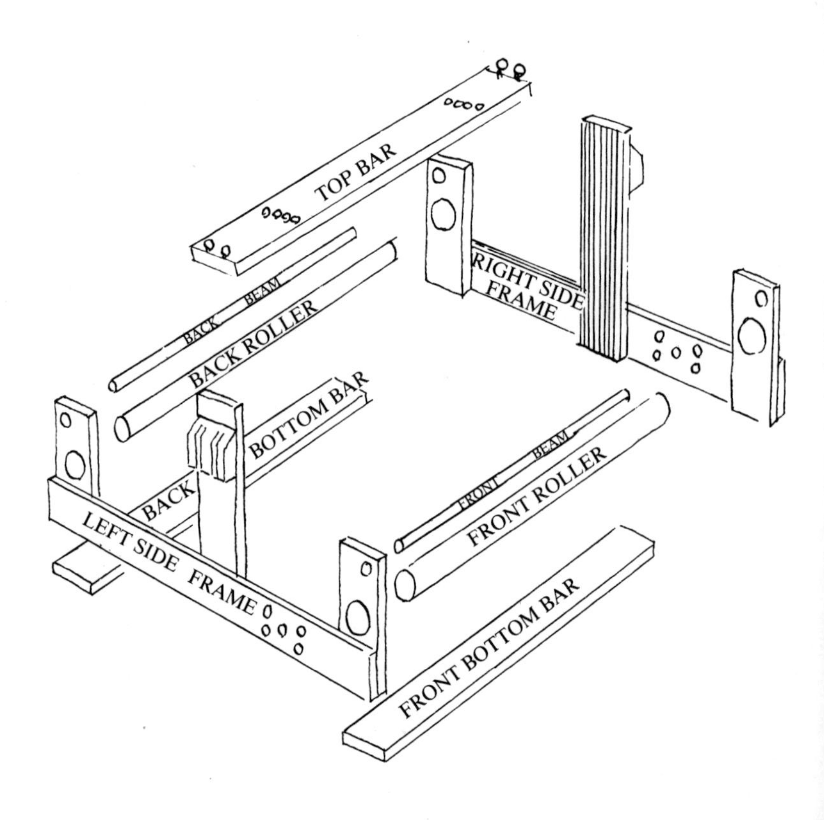

Figure 49. The basic components of the table loom.

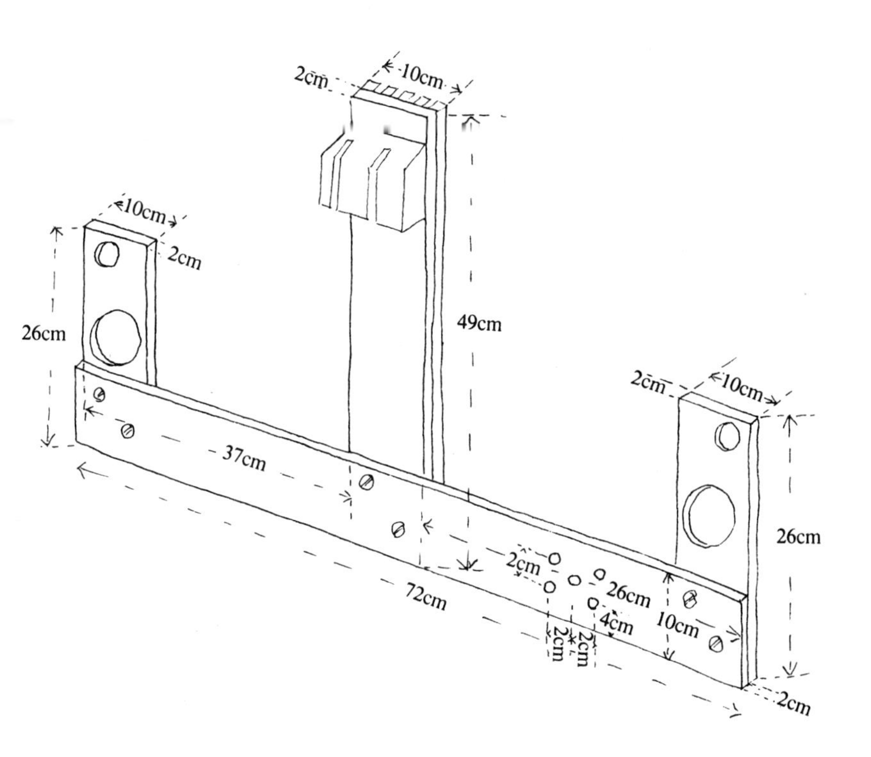

Figure 50. Dimensions of the side frames.

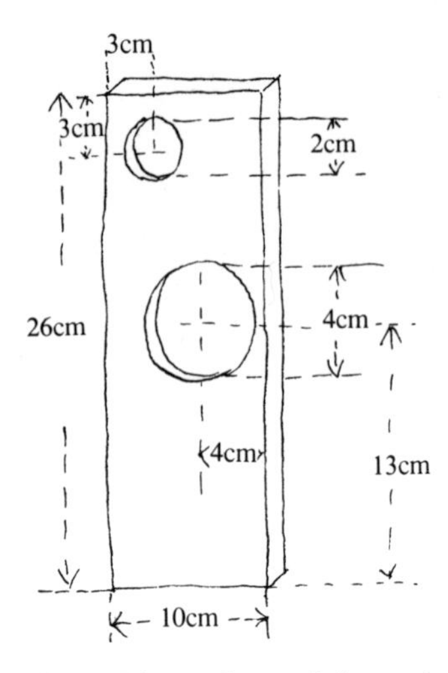

Figure 51. Dimensions of the end upright.

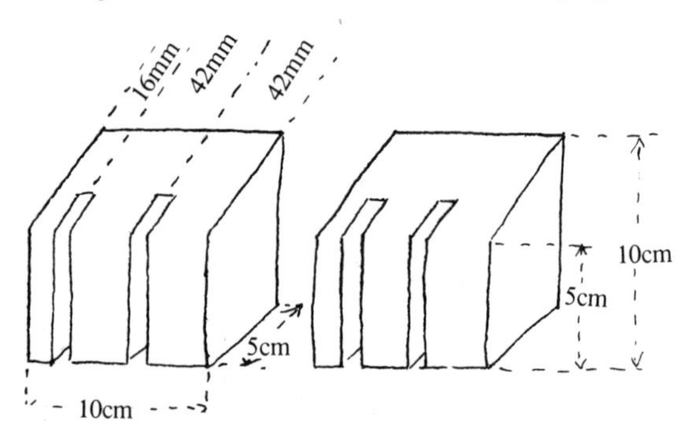

Figure 52. The lift blocks.

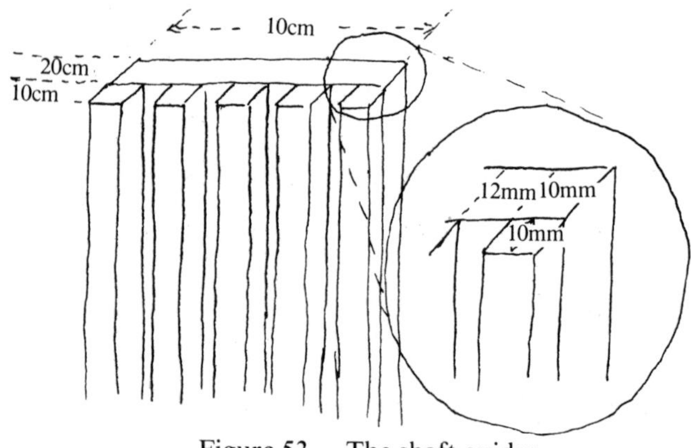

Figure 53. The shaft guides.

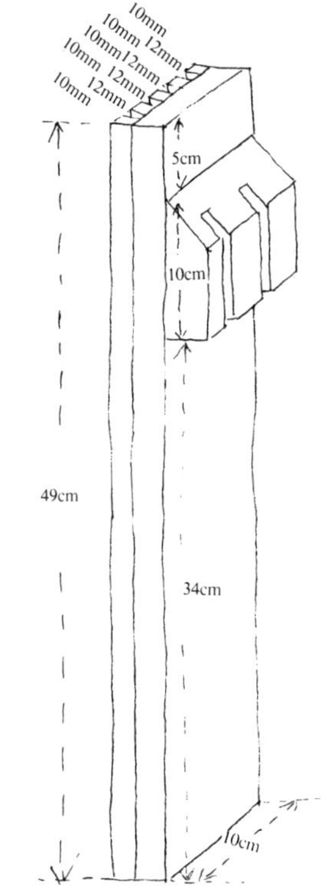

Figure 54. Dimensions of the central upright of the side frames.

Fixing the Two Side Frames
The two sides can now be fixed together. The front and back beams, both made from 2cm dowel and 54cm long should be glued in position as should the front and back bottom bars (58cm × 10cm × 2cm). Before fixing the top bar (54cm × 10cm × 2cm) drill four 5mm holes 10cm from each end (Figure 55) and fix two screw eyes in each end positioned as shown in Figure 59. Now glue and screw, the top bar in position.

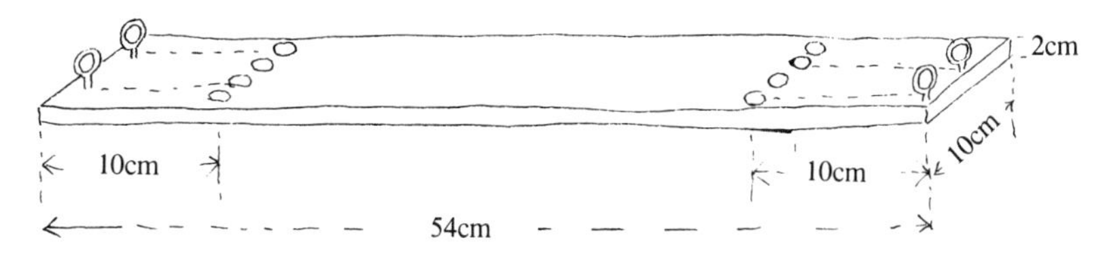

Figure 55. The top bar, showing the holes and eyelets.

Next, make the front and back rollers using 4cm dowel (thick broom handle). Both are 60cm long. Place them in their holes in the side frames and with 5cm protruding from the right side frame. Drill a 10mm hole through each end of the rollers just inside the side frames and stick a 6cm length of 10mm dowel through the holes as in Figure 56. This will hold the rollers in the loom and the basic frame is complete.

Drill three holes through the protruding ends of each roller (Figures 57 and 58) 10mm in diameter. Then fix two 4cm lengths of dowel into the bottom of the right side frame (Figures 59 and 60). By inserting a 20cm length of 10mm steel rod through the holes in the end of the roller and placing one end between the wooden dowels in the side frame the roller is held firm. By using a combination of different dowel pegs and roller holes the position of the roller can be varied (Figure 61).

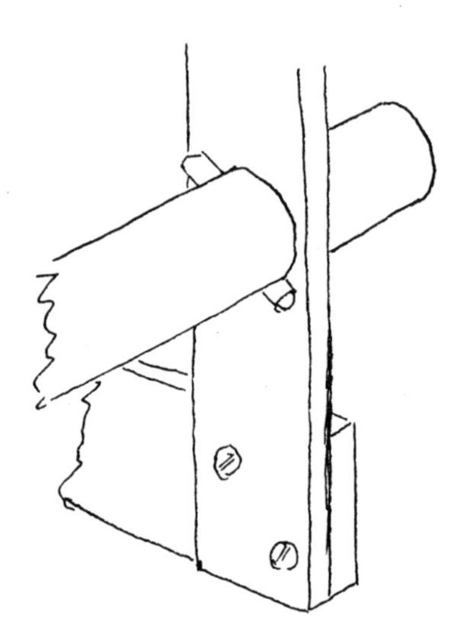

Figure 56. Position of front and back rollers in side frames, showing dowel on inside of frame.

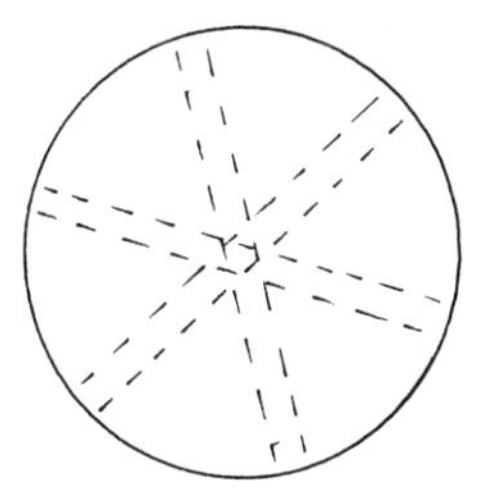

Figure 57. Three holes drilled through the protruding end of each roller.

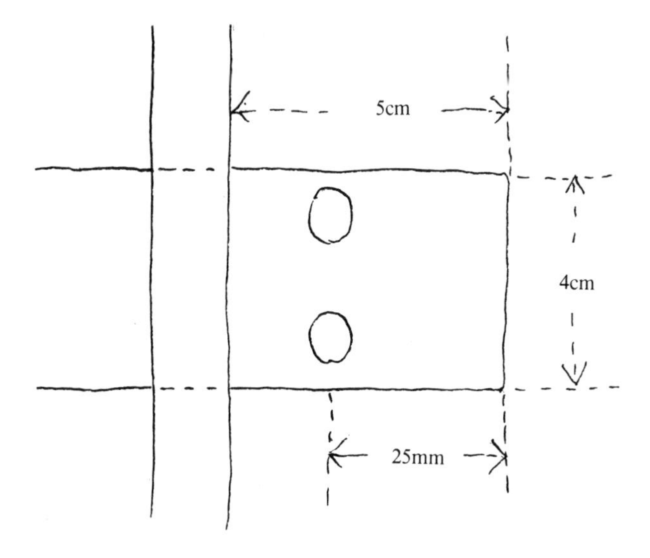

Figure 58. Position of the drilled holes in protruding end of roller.

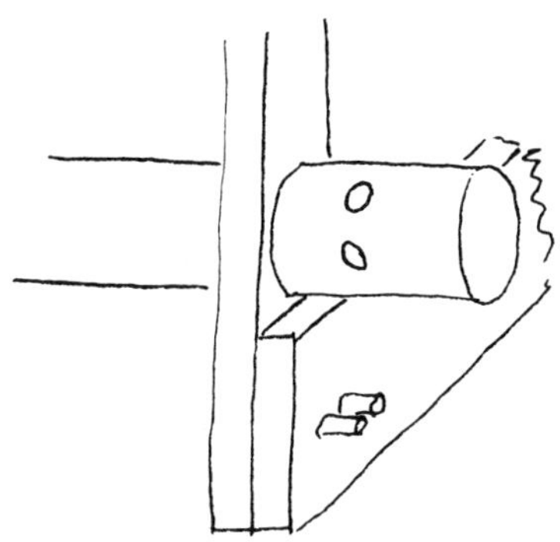

Figure 59. Position of the two pieces of dowel in the right side frame.

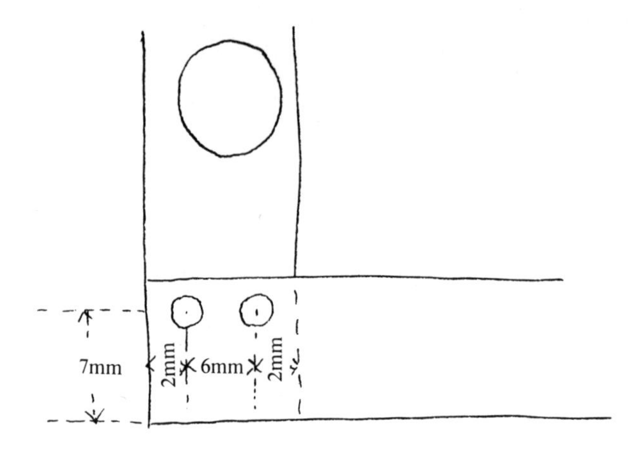

Figure 60. Dimensions of holes for the dowel, enabling variation of the roller position.

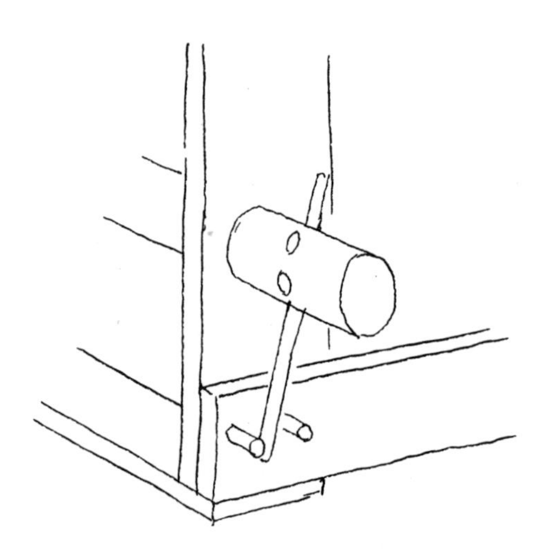

Figure 61. By a combination of different dowel pegs and roller holes the position of the roller can be varied.

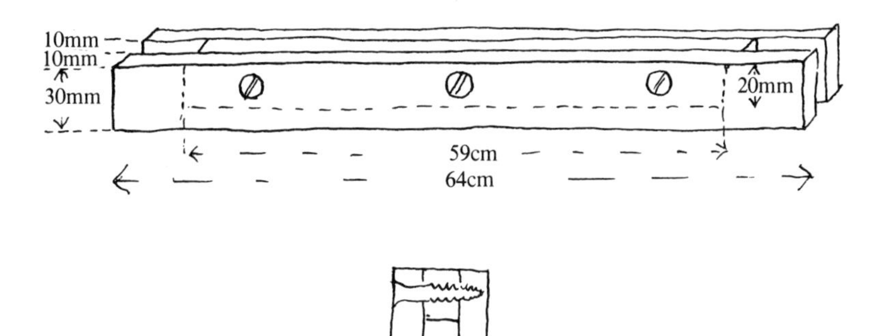

Figure 62. The moveable crosspiece of the batten.

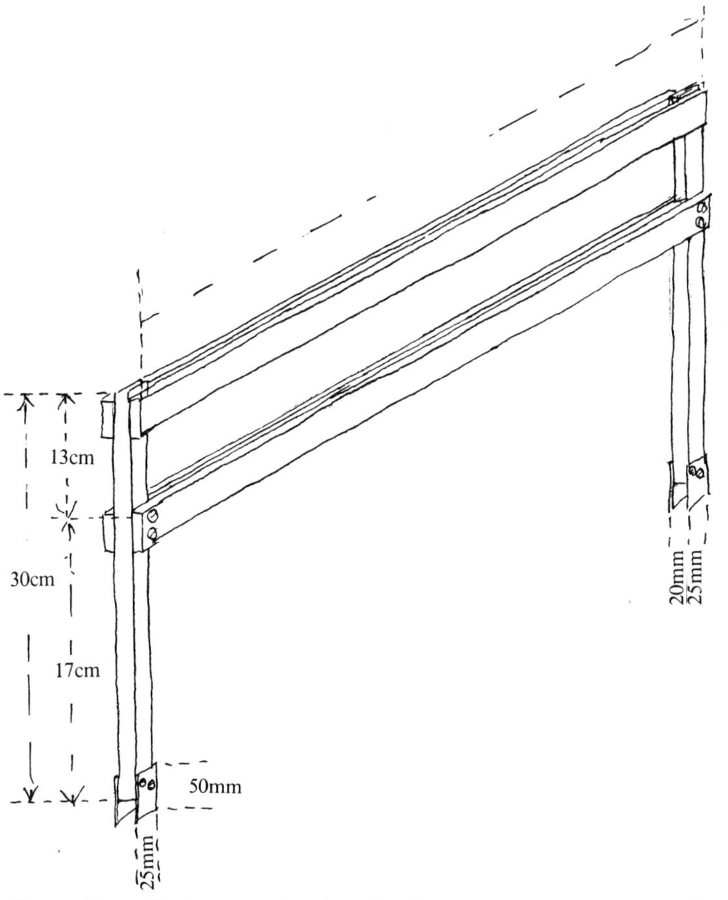

Figure 63. The batten, showing the fixed and moveable crosspiece.

The Batten

The batten (Figures 62 and 63) is rather like a set of rugby goal posts with an additional moveable crosspiece that slides up and down from the top. Between the two uprights and held in place between the fixed and moveable crosspieces rests the reed, a metal spacer like a comb. The whole batten rests on batten support pegs which protrude from the outside of the frame. These pegs are moveable to allow for vertical and horizontal adjustment of the batten, hence the five holes in each side frame to take these pegs (see Figure 50).

The uprights are 30cm × 25mm × 20mm with two metal plates 25mm × 50mm screwed onto the bottom of each upright (Figure 63).

The crosspieces are each made up of three pieces. Two pieces 64cm × 30mm × 10mm with a piece (59cm × 20mm × 10mm) sandwiched between them. The three pieces are screwed and glued together as in Figure 61 and the bottom crossbar is screwed and glued to the uprights with the groove uppermost, 13cm from the top. Ensure that the uprights and crossbar are at right angles to one another. The top crossbar is loose on the uprights and just slides up and down between them.

Next, drill five holes in the base of each side frame positioned as shown in Figure 50. Insert a 40mm length of dowel into matching holes and rest the batten upon them.

The Shaft and Heddles

These have nothing to do with mines or carts but are part of the system for raising and lowering threads. Shafts consist of heddles stretched between top and bottom shaft sticks. The shaft sticks are held in place by the shaft guides on the side frame. Each heddle has an eyelet at its centre. In order to weave, it is necessary to raise or lower these shafts. One does this by pulling down and fixing the handle into the lift block, thereby pulling on the cords which are attached to the top of the shaft by wire hooks (Figure 64). In order to assemble this last part of the loom you will need:

(1) Four pear shaped wooden handles 30mm diameter at the belly and drilled from top to bottom with a 3mm hole.
(2) Four top shaft sticks 400mm × 20mm × 10mm and four bottom shaft rods made of steel strip (available from D.I.Y. shops) also of 40cm × 20mm × 10mm.
(3) Four hundred heddles.

To make heddles knock four headless nails into a block of wood (Figure 65) and knot a length of heddle cord as illustrated. Heddle cord is a tightly twisted cotton yarn available from craft suppliers (see *Useful Information*) Use reef knots at A, B and C and an extra half knot at C. Turn on the radio and repeat the operation four hundred times.

Heddles are best tied up and removed from the nails in bundles of fifty. You will also need eight wire hooks and approximately five metres of strong linen or nylon cord. Craft suppliers sell loom cord for this purpose but look around and see what you can find.

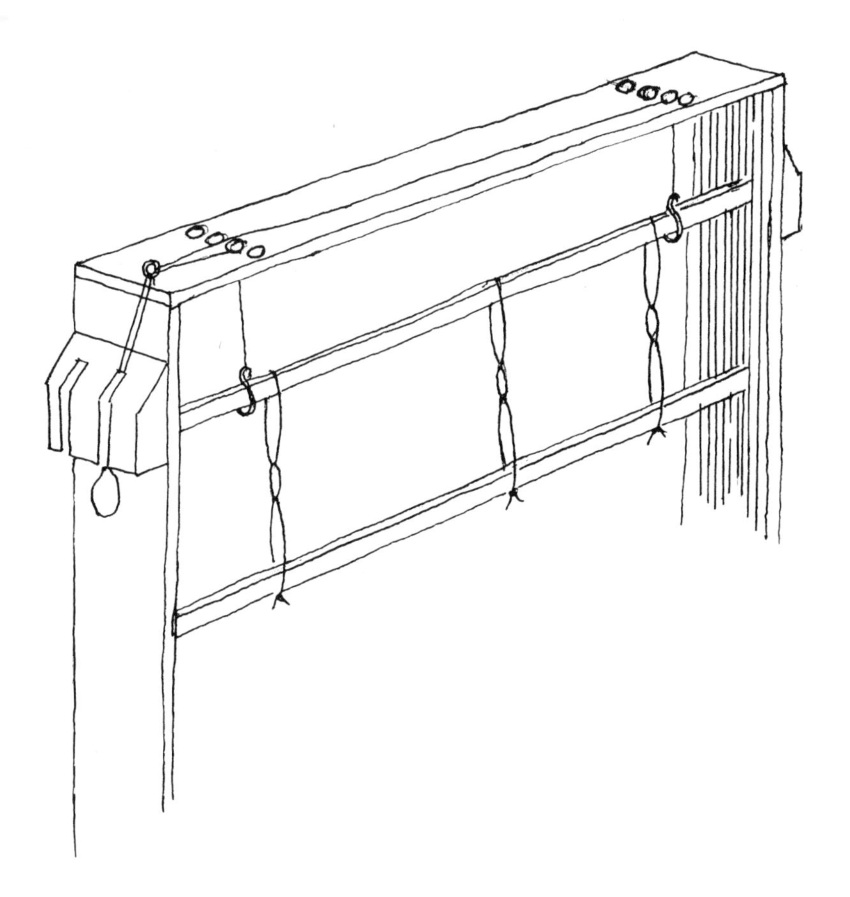

Figure 64. The shaft sticks and heddles.

Assembling a Shaft

To assemble a shaft, thread one hundred heddles onto a top shaft stick and a bottom shaft bar. Attach two wire hooks to the top stick 34cm apart. Tie on a 50cm length of cord to one hook and a 85cm length to the other. Thread these cords up through the holes in the top bar and out through one of the metal eyelets. Thread these two pieces of cord through one of the pear-shaped handles and knot to prevent the cord pulling out again. You will find that you can pull this handle down and slot it in beneath the lift block on the side of the loom. This will have the effect of raising the heddles in the shafts. Repeat the assembly operation for the other three shafts taking care to alternate the long and the short cords so that two handles rest on the left and two on the right of the loom. Finally cut four wooden rods from 10mm dowel each 60cm long. Round them off at the end. Two of these sticks are called cross sticks and in these drill 15mm holes 15mm from each end of both sticks. The other two sticks are the front

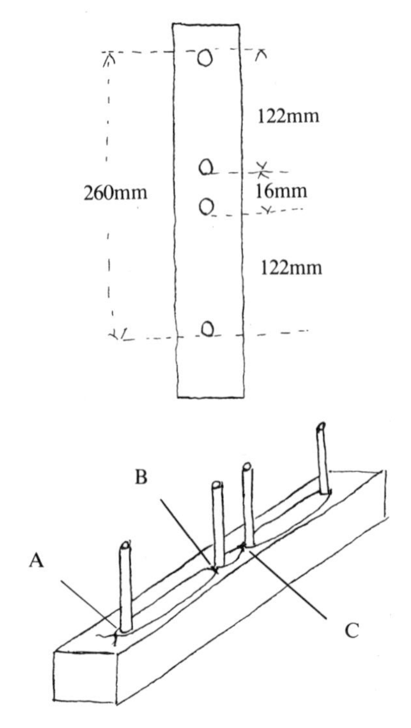

Figure 65. Dimensions of block of wood and nails used when knotting heddle cord.

and back warp sticks. More of these later—keep them all safe.

You will need to buy at least one reed or metal comb to fit between the crossbars on the batten. Ideally it is desirable to have quite a variety of reeds, each with a different number of teeth or 'dents' per cm centimetre, but they are expensive. A practical compromise would be to buy two reeds, one with ten dents per 3cm and the other with twelve dents per 3cm. Both reeds will need to be 50cm long.

So there you have it. A four shaft table loom made with your own fair hands. Have a look in loom-makers catalogues at the prices they ask for a similar sized loom and you will feel very satisfied.

7
THE FLOOR LOOM

The last piece of equipment to be described for you to make is a loom which stands on the floor and which can produce cloth up to 100cm wide. Compared to the table loom it is a hefty piece of equipment. There are a number of types of floor loom each with its distinctive way of operating. This loom is described as a counter-balanced loom. As you might guess with this type of loom the shafts are connected to each other in pairs on either side of the rollers balancing each other up (see Figure 78). The implication of this is that when one shaft is depressed then its partner is raised. This counter-balancing effect is the key characteristic of this kind of loom. It is useful to consider this proposed loom in terms of its differences to the table loom of the last chapter.

(1) Pedals are used instead of handles for raising and lowering the heddles.
(2) A batten pivoted from the top rather than the bottom.
(3) A counter-balanced type of harness.

The obvious advantage of this loom is that it can produce wider cloth but it is also faster to operate. The reason for this is that on a table loom all the manipulating of threads or loom has to be done by the hands. With a floor loom this work is shared out between the feet and hands and so the process is quicker.

Disadvantages
It is only fair to consider the disadvantages. First, of course, is its

size and weight. Unlike the table loom it cannot be tucked away out of sight when not in use. You need a permanent site for it—a space about two metres square with walking space all around it. You also need good lighting. The ideal is a large north facing window, augmented by a strip light overhead. You will be particularly aware of the need for good lighting when you are working with dark blue or black thread.

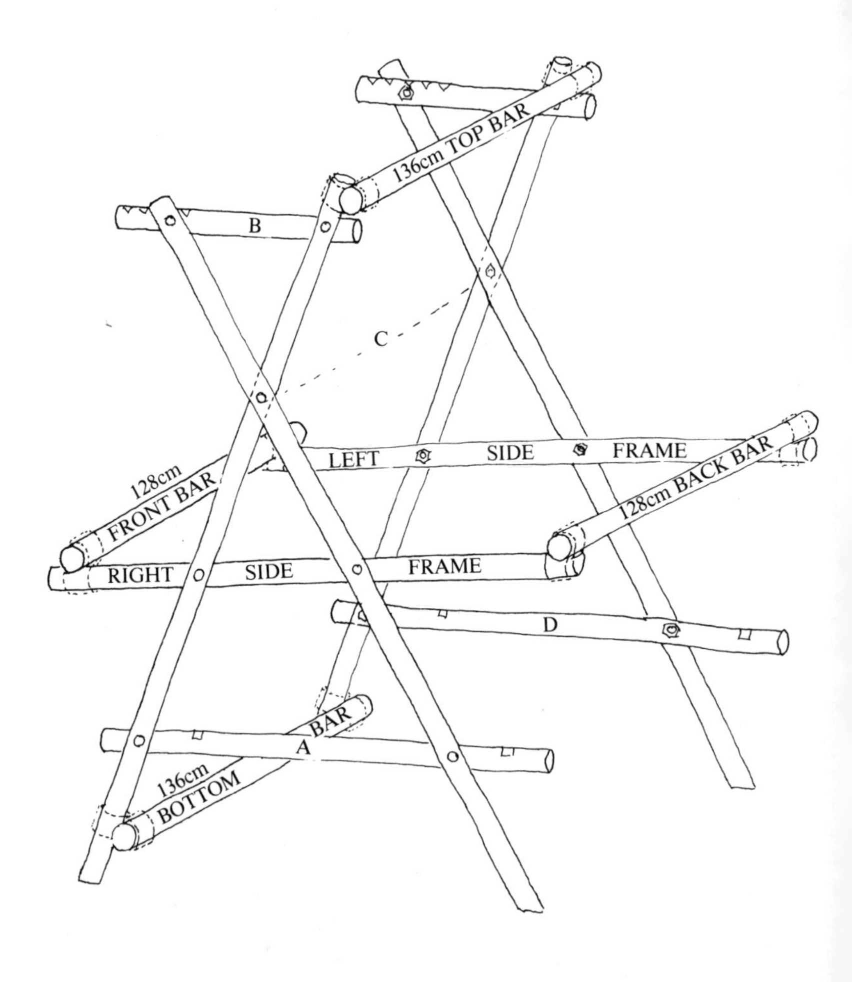

Figure 66. The basic frame of the floor loom.

Similarities with the Table Loom

Provided you have the space and light, a floor loom is a great improvement over a table loom. This floor loom has exactly the same elements as the table loom described in the previous chapter:

(1) A roller at each end—one to hold the warp, the other to hold the cloth.
(2) Heddles with eyes, through which the warp passes, supported in an arrangement to raise or lower them.
(3) A batten and reed to space the warp thread apart and to beat the weft threads up tight.
(4) A frame to hold all these parts in the correct positions relative to each other

Frame Specifications

I will start with the specifications for the frame. It is made almost entirely from steel tube scaffolding rejected by the building trades. By visiting builders or scrap yards you should be able to get the amount you want at reasonable prices. The reason that scaffolding becomes available at all is that once a length of scaffolding is bent its strength is greatly reduced and it is no longer of use as building scaffolding. No reputable builder ever takes chances with his scaffolding for it is required to support great weights of building material and a bent or weak pipe could cause a catastrophic collapse. So go searching for rejected and bent lengths of tube which can be cut into the short lengths you need for the frame of this loom.

Figure 66 shows the frame. You will see that it is made up of two side frames joined by four cross bars. Figure 67 shows one side frame. Make up the two sides. The joint at point C needs to be made as in Figure 68 using a 15mm × 50mm bolt and nut while all other joints can be made as in Figure 69 using 15mm × 90mm bolts and nuts. After tightening all joints cut off any excess length of bolt.

The two sides are now joined together with the front and back bars (128cm long) and the top and bottom bars (136cm long). They are clamped to the side frames with scaffolding clamps. There are a considerable number of different designs of clamp in use so I have left the illustration (Figure 66) deliberately vague. The only specifications are that they should fit the scaffolding pipe you are using and that they can be tightened to give a rigid frame.

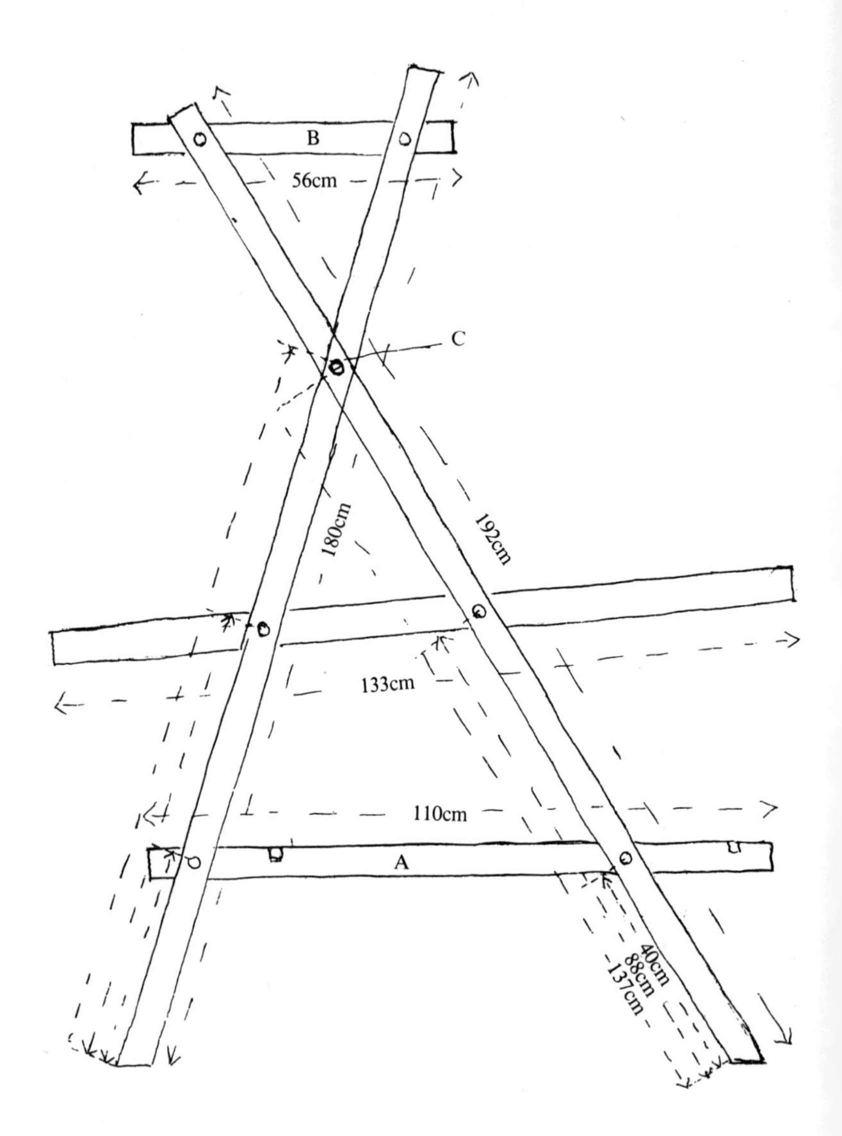

Figure 67. A side frame.

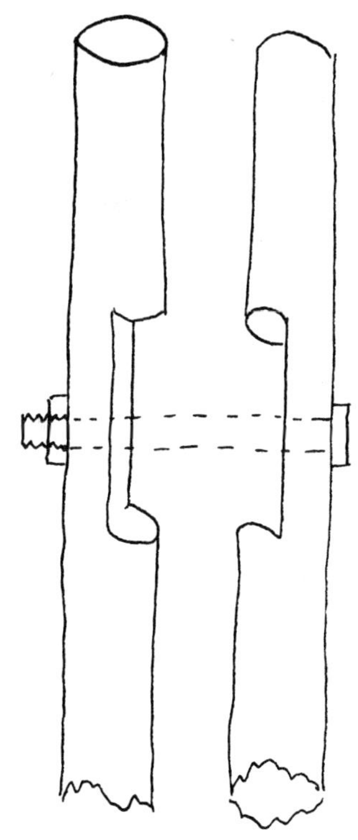

Figure 68. The arrangement of the joint at point C.

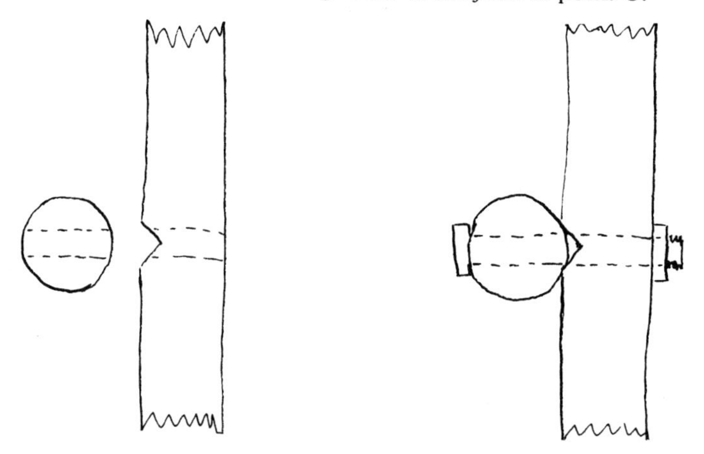

Figure 69. The arrangement of all side frame joints other than at point C.

Before proceeding further it would be well to give the frame a good rub down with a wire brush followed by a coat of metal primer.

The Pedal Assembly

Figure 70 shows the pedal assembly and Figures 71, 72 and 73 show the dimensions of the wooden blocks, rod, pedal and washers. The 4cm washers placed between each pedal can be made of either blocks of wood with a 15mm hole drilled through them or of 4cm lengths of suitable pipe. When the pedals and washers have been threaded onto the rod, it is glued into the blocks and pinned with a nail. The assembly then fits under the bottom bar but is not fixed firm to it.

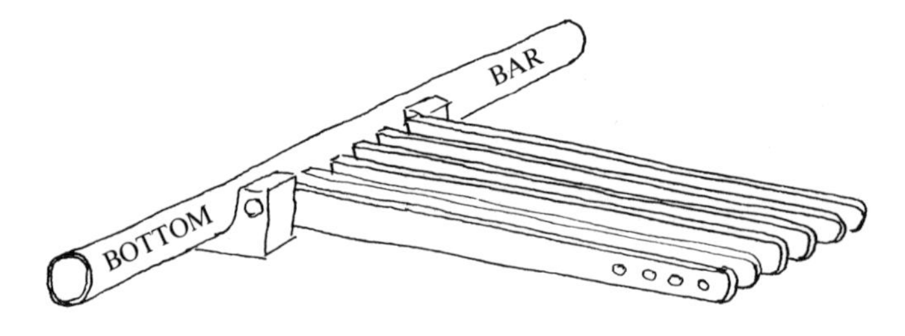

Figure 70. The pedal assembly.

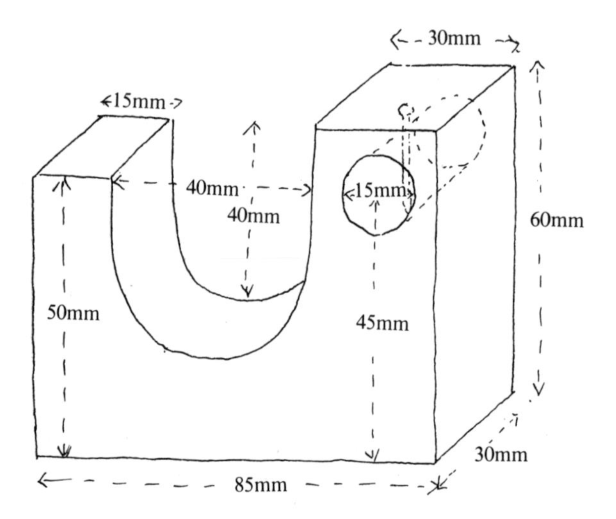

Figure 71. The dimensions of the wooden blocks in the pedal assembly.

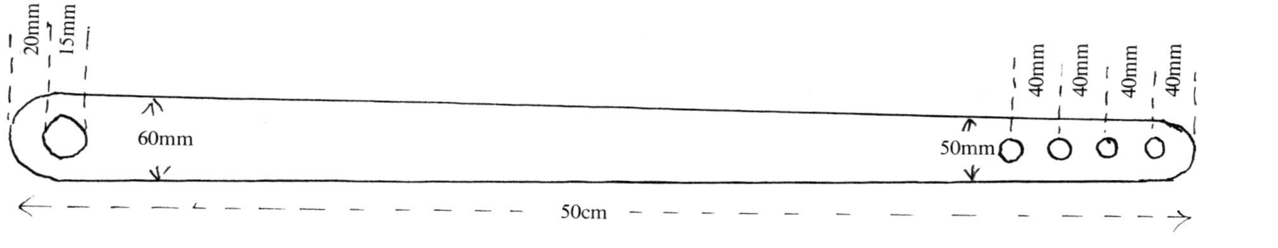

Figure 72. The dimensions of the pedal.

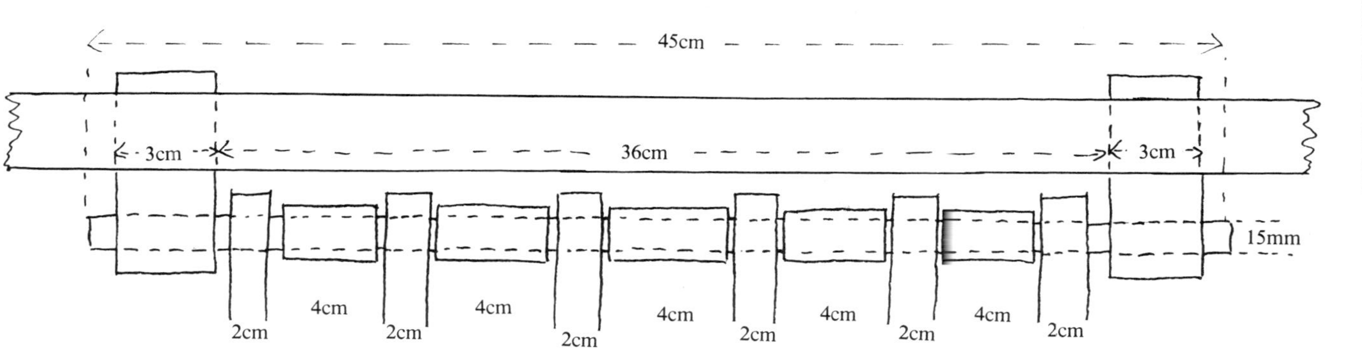

Figure 73. The positions of the wooden blocks, rod, pedal, and washers in the pedal assembly.

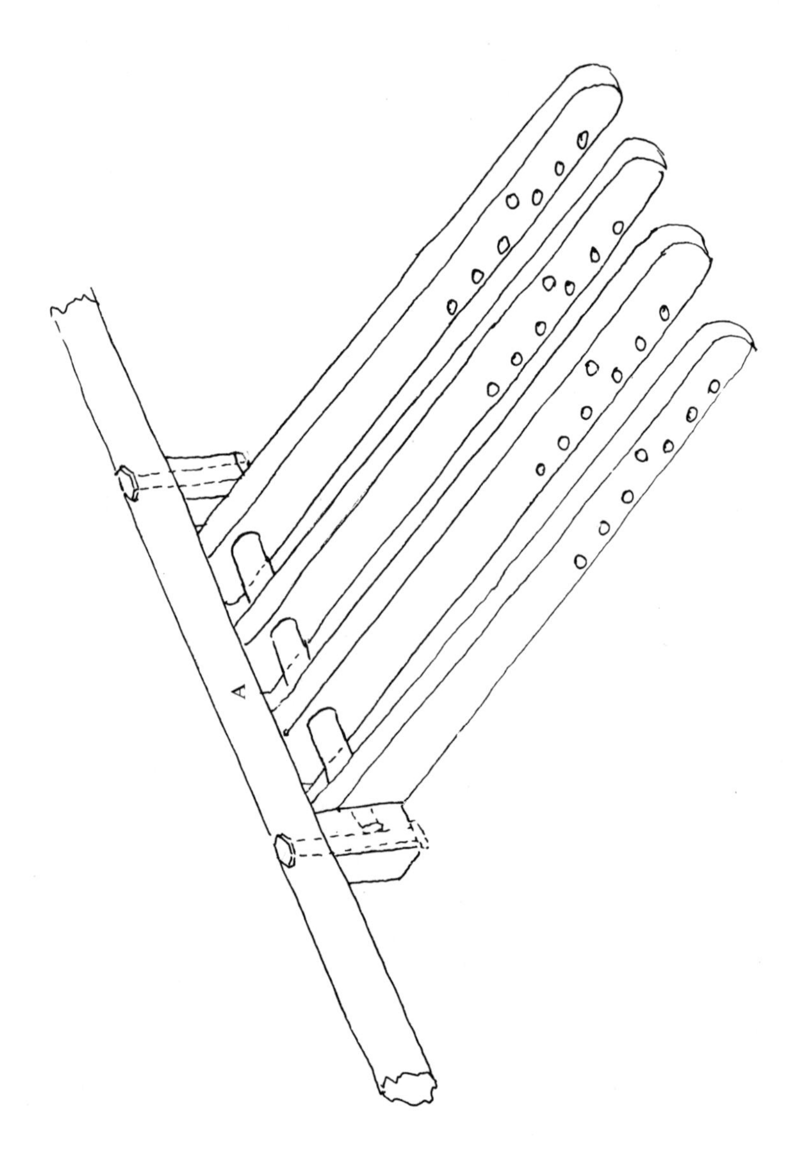

Figure 74. The Lamms.

The Lamms

The Lamms (Figure 74) are a somewhat similar set of four pieces of wood pivoted on a rod supported beneath the right side frame bar A. The dimensions are shown in Figures 75, 76 and 77. You will notice that the support blocks are curved on top so that they fit snugly beneath bar A and are held in place by 150mm × 10mm bolts and nuts.

The Harness

Figure 78 shows the harness. This is the arrangement for lowering or raising the eyelets through which the warp threads pass. You will see that it is made up of two layers of rollers which support the shafts and below them the Lamms. Figure 79 shows the method of attaching the top roller to the top bar. The metal pins in either end of the top roller are 7mm × 100mm bolts with the heads hacksawed off (Figure 80). Drill the ends of the rollers and glue the bolts in with Araldite. Those for the lower rollers are made from similar bolts but with the heads left on (Figure 81). Before fixing the bolts in the lower rollers, slide a metal plate (Figure 82) onto the bolts. Drill and glue the bolts in place. The shafts and rollers are hung on lengths of nylon cord and you will notice that these cords make a turn and a half around the roller above them.

The Heddles

The heddles are made up in exactly the same way as those described in the previous chapter but they are larger, 40cm from top to bottom. Make up a block as described in the previous chapter but with the larger dimensions. You will need 800 heddles, 200 for each shaft. They are made of heddle cord which can be purchased from weaving equipment suppliers. When you have hung the harness adjust the cords so that the eyelets of the heddles are in an imaginary line between the tops of the front and back bars. The Lamms should be parallel to the floor.

The Batten

Next item to make is the batten. You will see that it is similar to the one made for the table loom in the previous chapter, but that this one hangs from the top rather than pivoting from the bottom. Figure 83 shows the dimensions and Figure 84 is a detailed drawing of the ends of the batten support bar. The wedge shaped ends of the batten support bar are protected by a

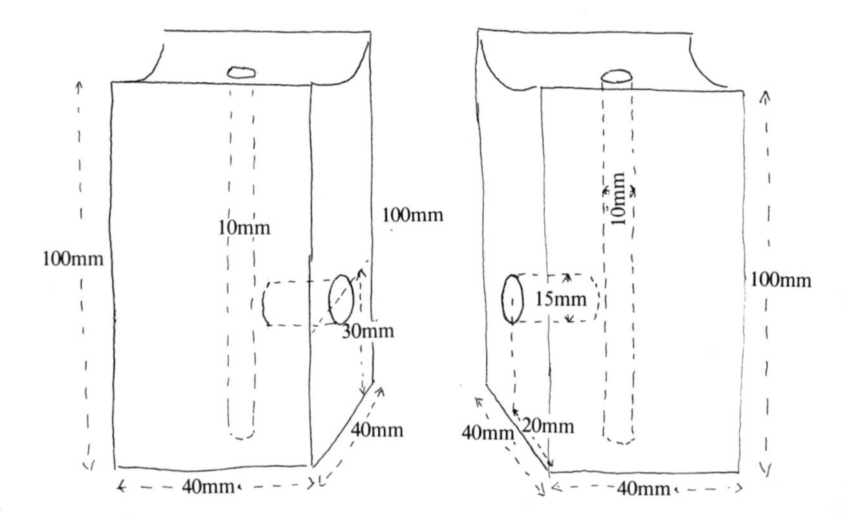

Figure 75. The dimensions of the curved support blocks of the Lamms.

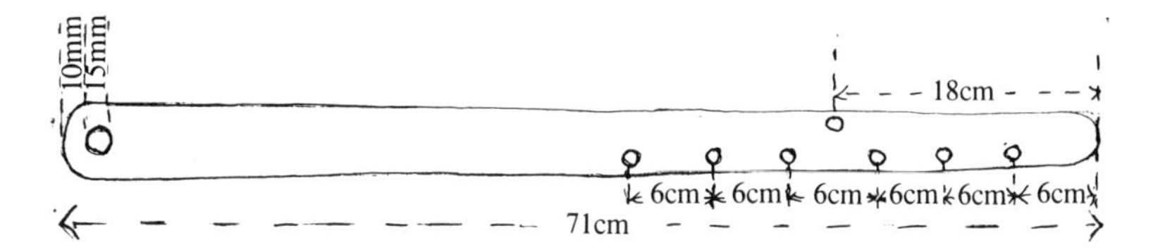

Figure 76. The dimensions of the wood struts and position of holes.

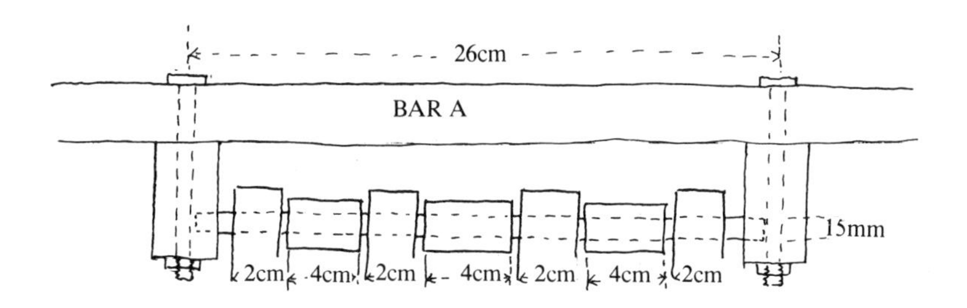

Figure 77. The positions of the support blocks, the rod, struts and washers of the Lamms.

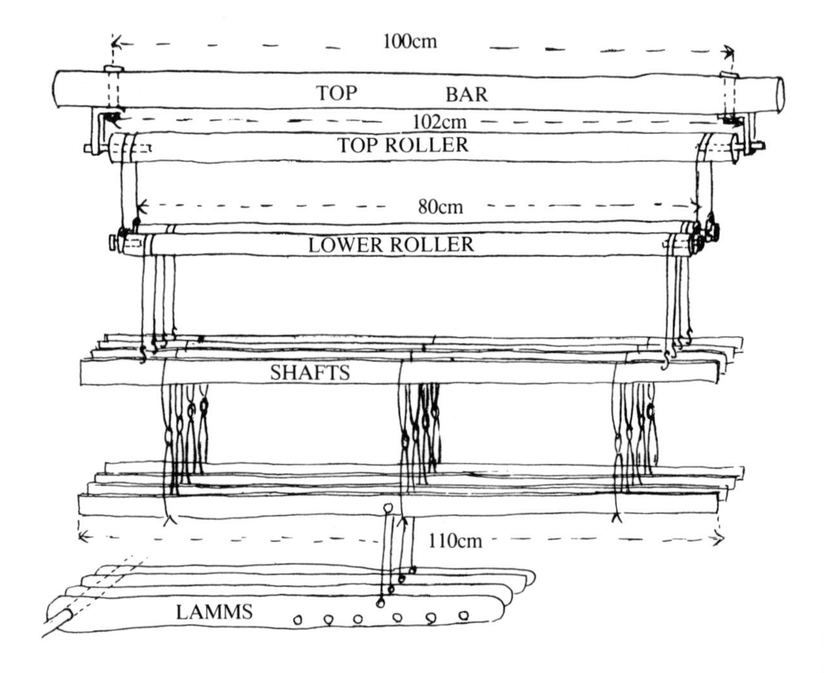

Figure 78. The harness.

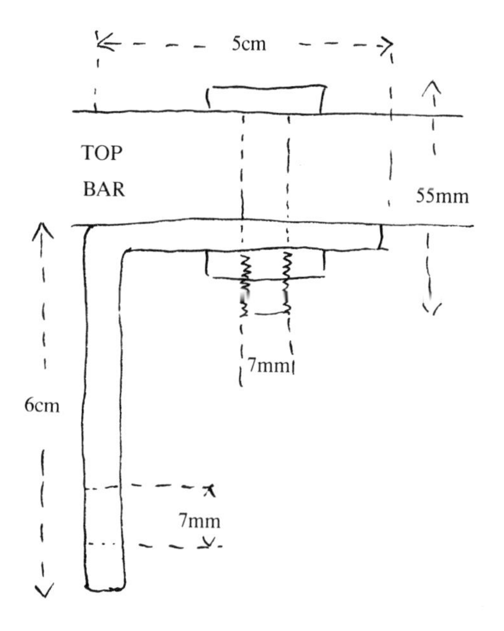

Figure 79. Method of attaching the top roller to the top bar.

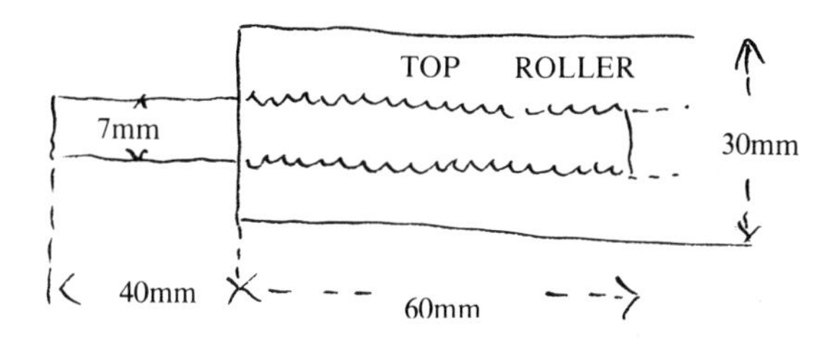

Figure 80. The metal pins in the top roller are bolts with the heads hacksawed off.

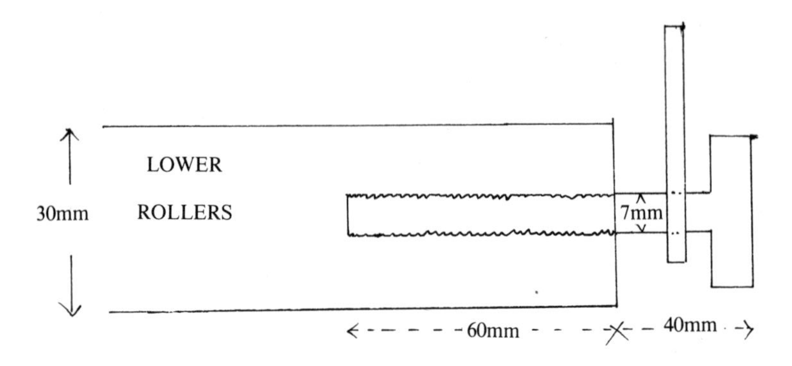

Figure 81. The bolt heads remain on the lower roller pins.

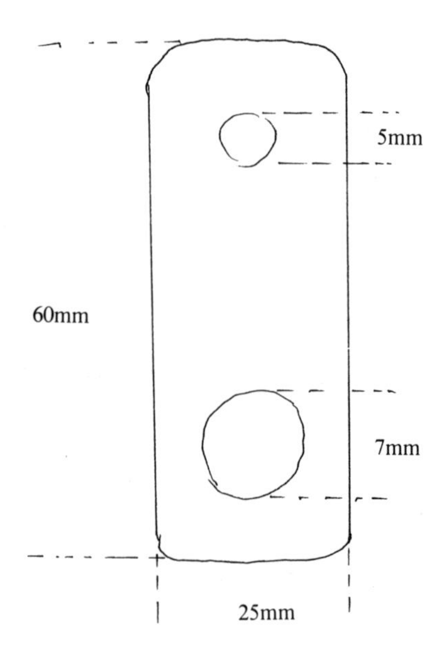

Figure 82. Dimensions of a metal plate to be slid onto the lower roller bolts.

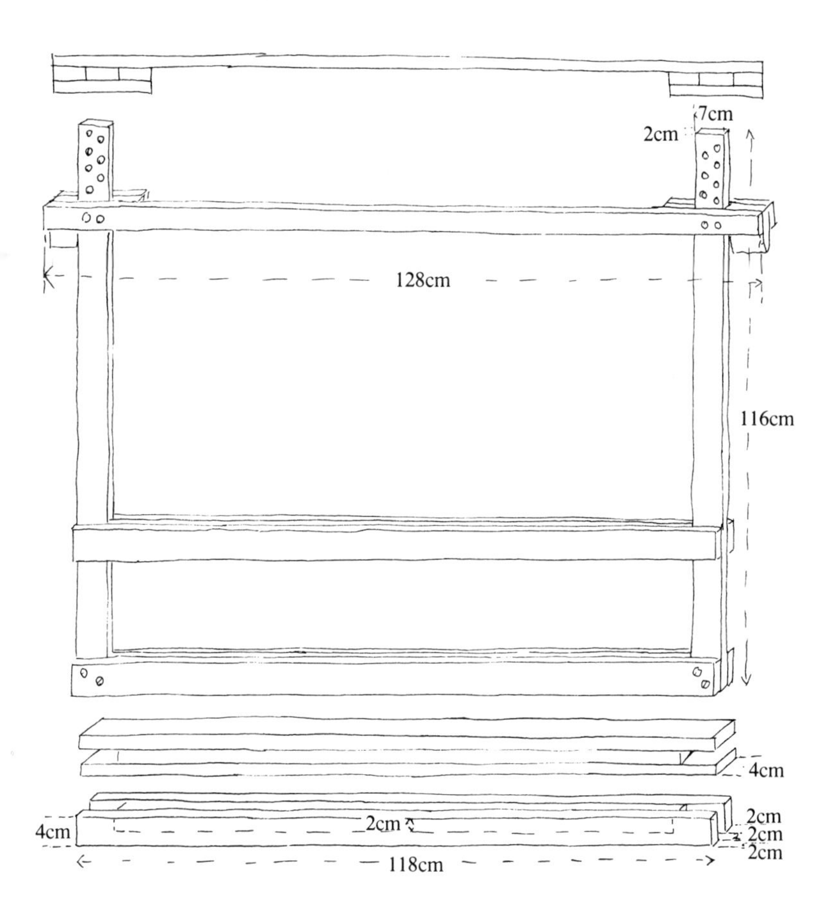

Figure 83. Dimensions of the batten

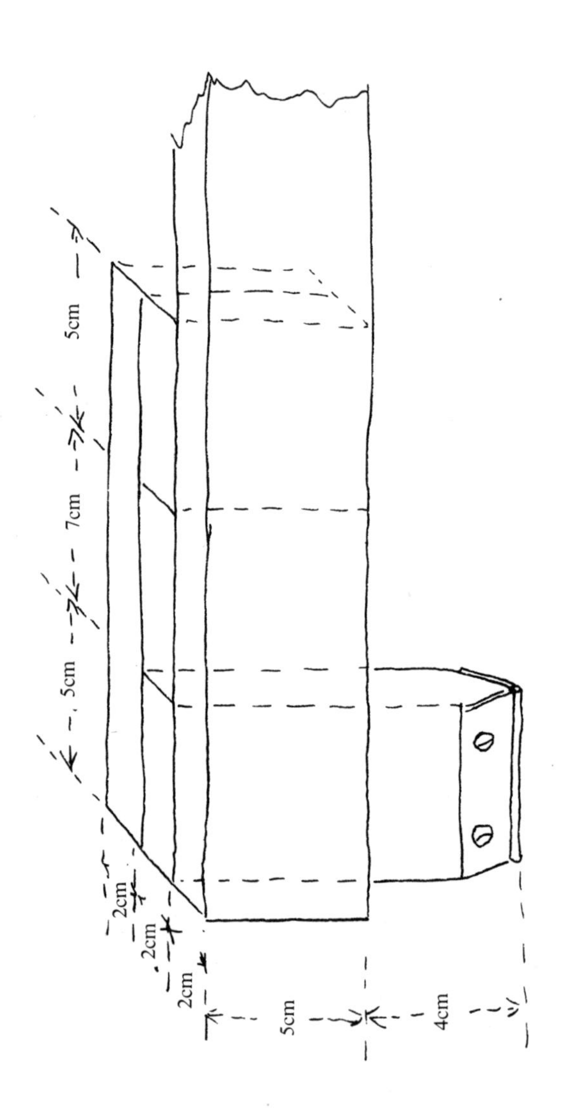

Figure 84. Detailed drawing of the ends of the batten support bar.

small brass hinge which helps to reduce wear. The top bars of both side frames should now have a series of five V-shaped cuts made in them with a hacksaw (see Figure 66) to take these wedge-shaped supports. The cuts should be 2cm apart and approx. 10mm deep. Wooden pegs 5cm long are placed through the holes in the batten support and the batten uprights. The height of the batten in the loom can be altered by using higher or lower holes in the supports. The batten now swings in the frame.

The Rollers

The last item to add to the loom are the rollers. Both front and back rollers are identical and Figures 85, 86 and 87 show the dimensions. You will notice that the rollers are not round and are made up of a number of pieces of wood joined together. Cloth or threads can be wound around these rollers just as they would on round rollers, and they have the advantage of being cheaper and easier to make. Before glueing the metal axles into the rollers make a number of small cuts in the metal which will be inserted. This allows the glue to get a much better grip on the rod. Each roller has a handle attached on the right and a cog-wheel attached on the left. The handles, which are made from two pieces of wood 40mm × 30mm × 45cm, are jointed at the centre and drilled with a 20mm hole. Both ends of both pieces are shaped into handles (Figure 88). The handles are fixed to the left hand end of the roller with four angle irons. The cog-wheel, which is cut from two layers of 15mm ply glued together, is also fixed to the roller with four angle irons (Figure 89). This wheel is fixed with the square face of each cog facing towards the front of the loom over the top of the roller (Figure 90).

The rollers are held in the loom with a pivoting plate fixed over a cut in the frame (Figure 91). The cuts are 20mm deep and 10mm wide and positioned 8cm from the back and 22cm from the front of the two bottom side frame bars. (See A and D, Figure 66.) A metal plate 20mm × 50mm is cut and drilled as in Figure 92. It is fixed with two 50mm × 5mm bolts and nuts.

The long wooden rachets must be fixed to the frame to control the rotation of the rollers. Both are the same size and shape (Figure 93) and are attached to the inside of the right hand side frame bar A as shown in Figure 94 using a 10mm bolt 75mm long. Figure 94 applies to both front and back rollers.

Lastly knock in three large staples positioned as in Figure 87. Attach a 2m length of strong cord, doubled over, to each staple

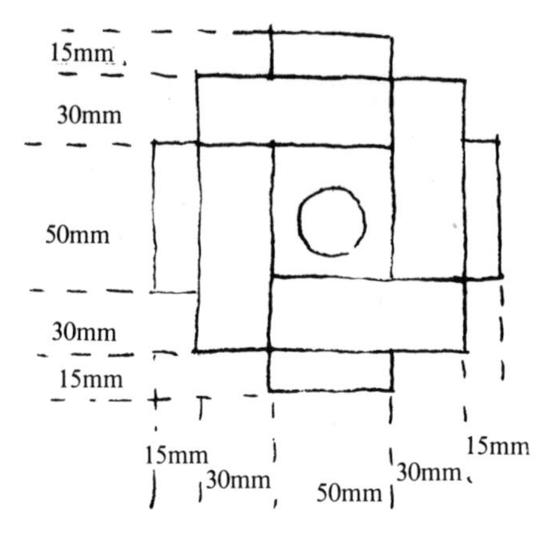

Figure 85. Cross section of the front or back roller.

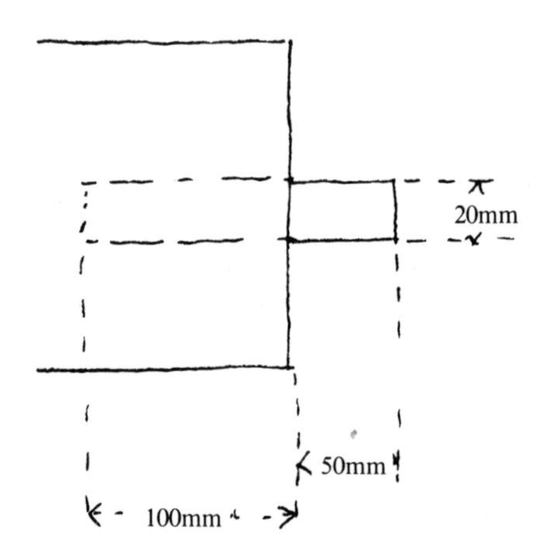

Figure 86. The metal axle of the front or back roller.

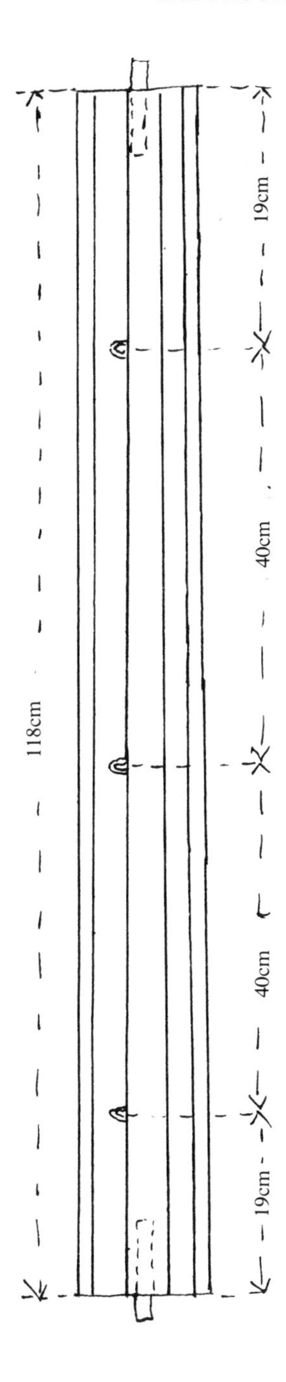

Figure 87. Front view of a roller, showing the position of the staples.

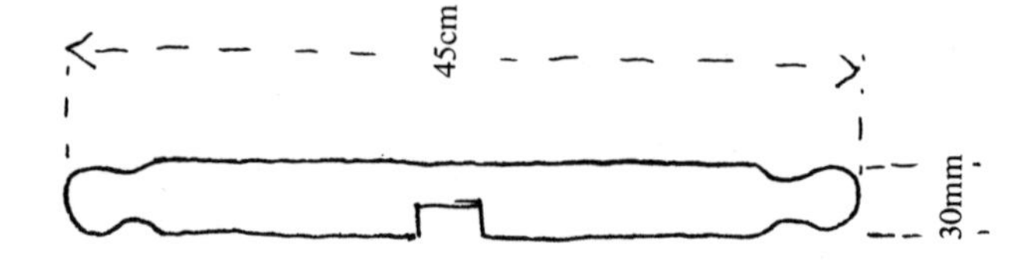

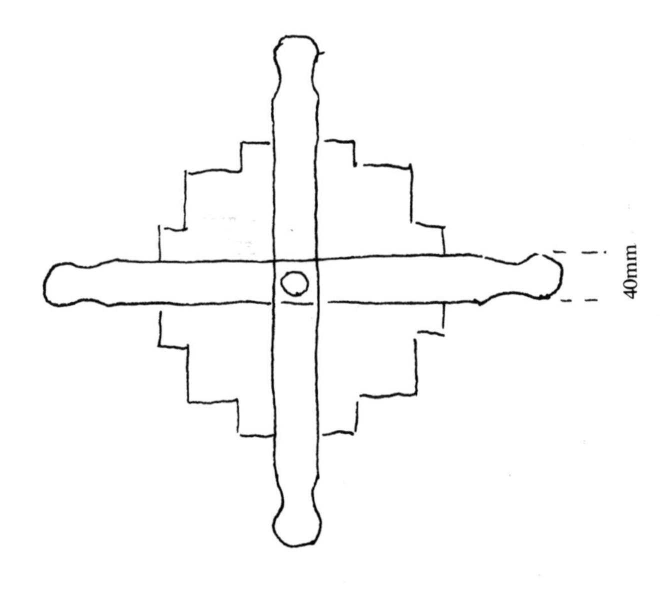

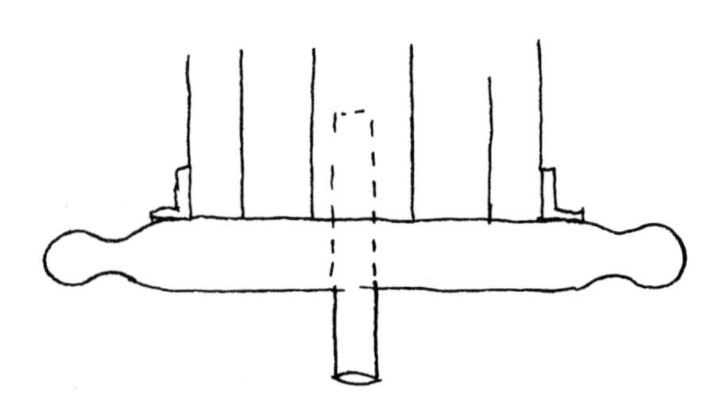

Figure 88. The handles on one end of each roller.

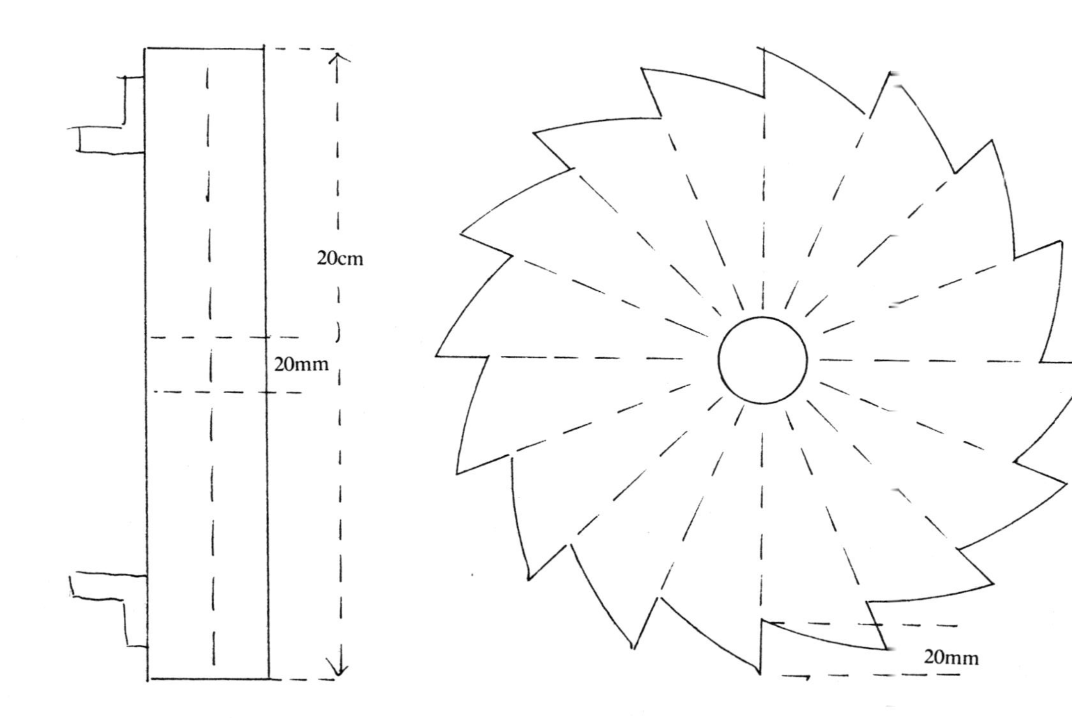

Figure 89. The cog-wheel on the other end of each roller.

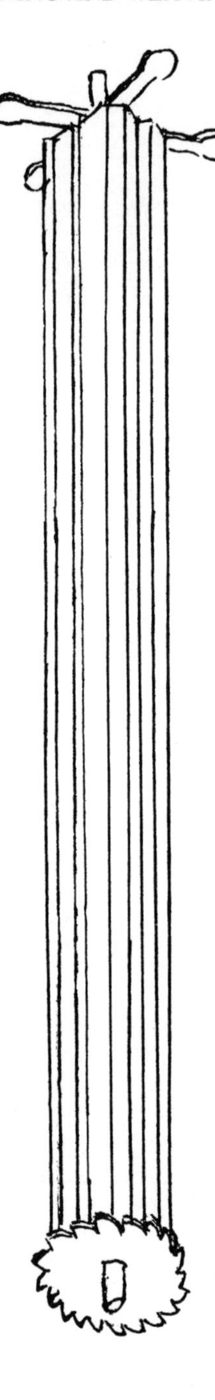

Figure 90. The completed roller.

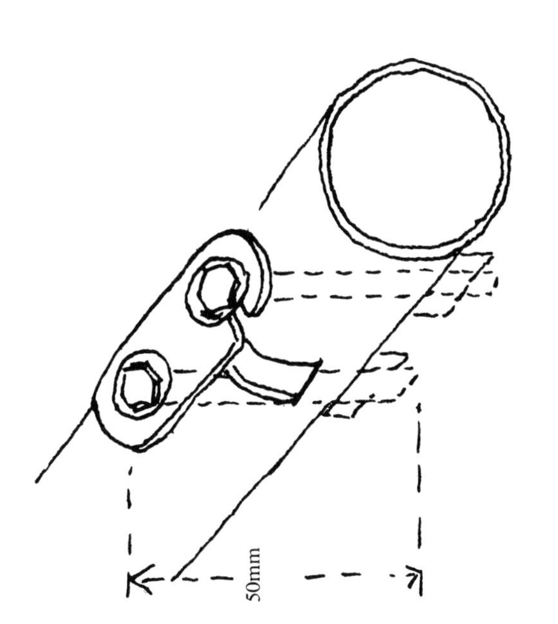

Figure 91. Pivoting plate fixed over a cut in the frame for securing the rollers.

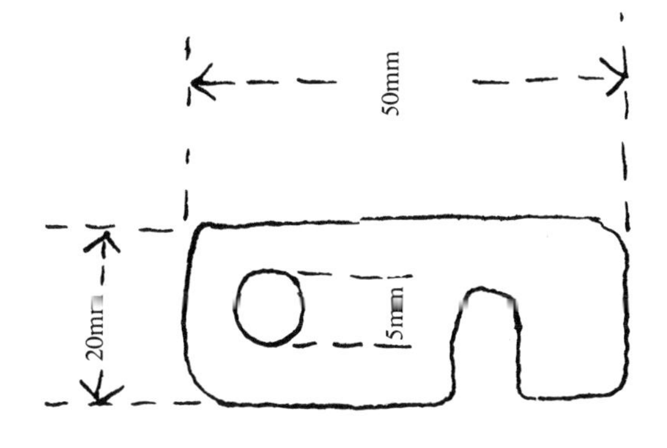

Figure 92. The dimensions of the pivoting plate.

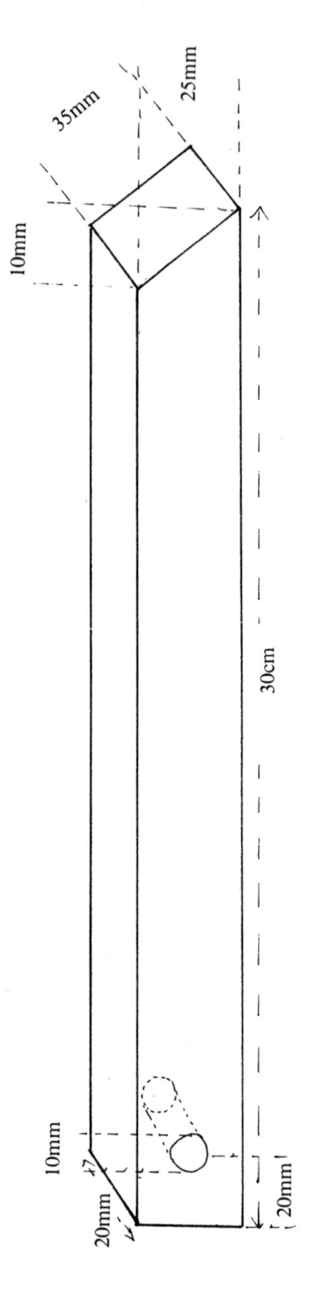

Figure 93. Dimensions of the wooden rachets.

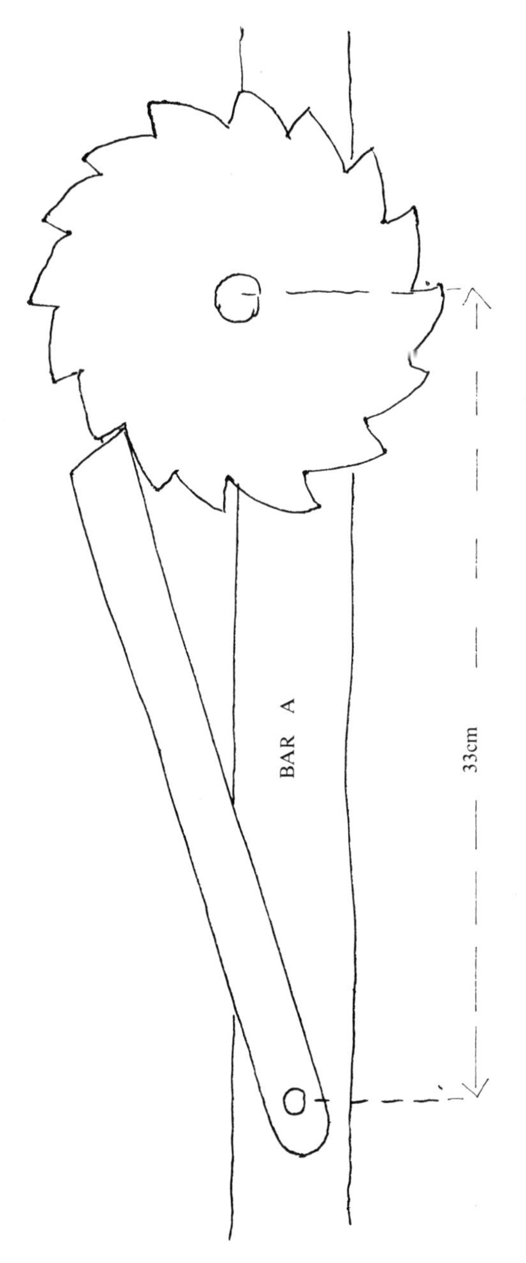

Figure 94. The position of the rachets on the frame.

with these cords tie a 100cm length of 15mm wooden dowel to each roller.

Extras

There are a few extras you will need. Two cross sticks—125cm lengths of 30mm × 10mm wood with 3mm holes drilled 10mm from each end—two or three roller shuttles and at least two reeds. The shuttles for a loom of this width are boat-shaped pieces of wood with rollers in the centre. They are tricky things to make and you would do best to buy them from a weaving equipment supplier. The reeds also are something you should buy. You will need two reeds at least—one with 10 dents in 25mm and the other 12 dents in 25mm. Both must be 100cm long.

To finish the loom and give it a bit of class (after all, it is made largely of junk) paint the scaffolding pipe with matt black paint and give all the wooden parts two coats of varnish. You might like to whittle some nice wooden pegs to fill all the ends of the pipes and prevent spiders making their homes in them. Compared with the usual all-wood looms, this one is heavy and, to be honest, a bit clumsy, but it is strong and it will work.

If you feel you might have done better to have bought a comparable loom from a supplier just patch up your scarred hands with elastoplast, look up the prices in a catalogue and then spend the money saved on a large and varied selection of yarns to start you on your weaving career.

8
FINAL TIPS

Figure 95 is a simplified diagram of the main parts of a loom. You will remember that a loom consists of three elements.

(1) The rollers, one at each end of the loom. The warp threads are stored on one and the woven cloth on the other. The warp is stretched between them. The warp threads are kept in order by the alternating of the threads between the cross sticks.

(2) The heddles with eyelets through which threads pass and which are raised or lowered by the harness. In a table loom this harness is moved by handles. On the floor loom it is moved by rollers, Lamms and pedals.

(3) A batten and reed which serves to spread the warp threads evenly across the width of the warp and which also compresses the weft thread into the cloth.

Weaving consists of using the functions of these three elements in a certain sequence. First by raising or lowering some of the heddles an opening is made in the warp threads. A weft thread is then passed through this opening so as to interlace it at right angles to the warp. The opening is then shut and the thread trapped close to the cloth. A new and different opening is then made in the warp threads and another weft thread is passed through it. The sequence is repeated and a cloth emerges.

Making the Most of Weaving

The process of putting a warp on a loom, crossing it with a weft

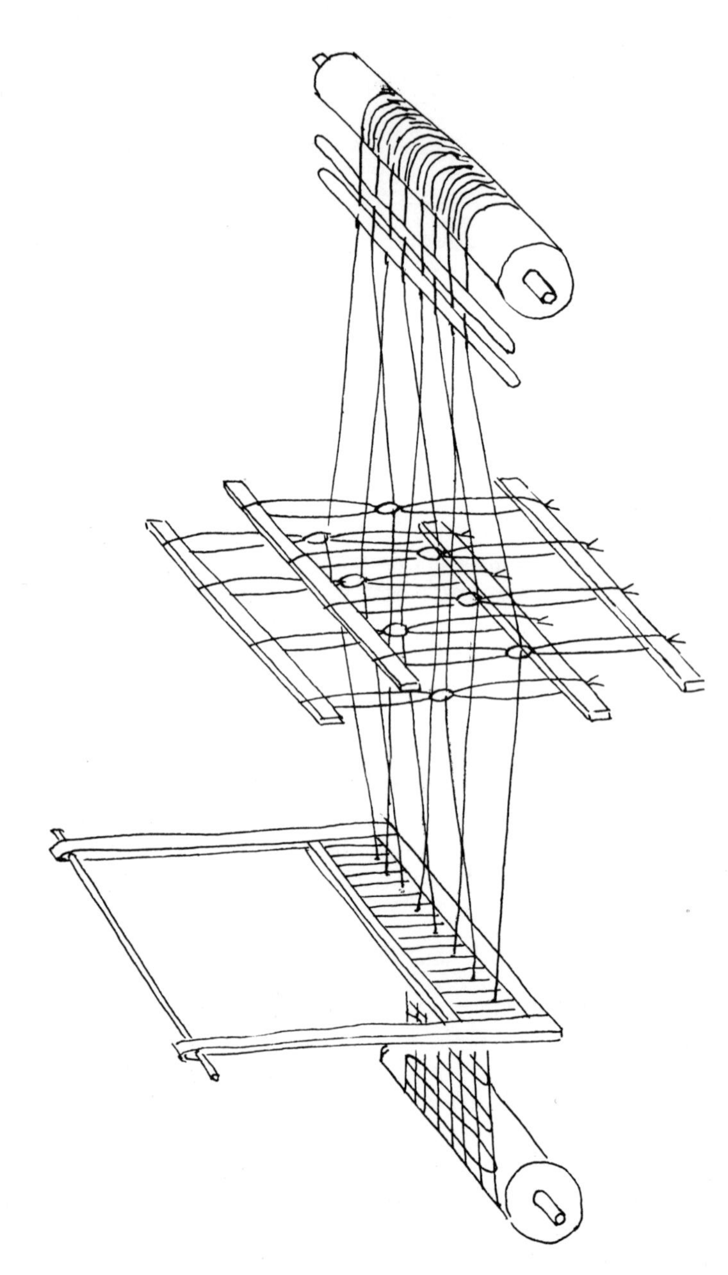

Figure 95. Simplified diagram of the main working parts of the floor loom.

and thereby producing a piece of cloth is at the same time both simple and complex. The basic task of producing a cloth by interlacing two sets of threads at right angles to each other is the simple one. What can make it complicated is that within these objectives almost limitless variations are possible—variation in the size, colour, texture, and composition of the threads used. There can also be variation in the sequence of interlacing those threads. These two sets of variables make possible an almost limitless series of combinations.

At the same time, of course, there are limitations. The competence of the weaver, the availability of raw material or the shortcomings of the equipment—all these things impose some measure of control upon the weaver. Becoming a competent weaver is the task of understanding and using all these limitations and possibilities to your own advantage.

It is a two-part task, a weaver must be part designer or artist and part technician or mechanic. Both parts are of equal importance, so when choosing books or courses of instruction look to both aspects.

To guide you through this whole process of discovery is beyond the scope of this book, or indeed, of any single book. For those who get bitten by the weaving bug it will be a life-long journey of discovery and well worth the effort too!

Fleeces

A great variety of fibres can, and have, been spun into thread—anything from nettles to the cost of the musk ox. Endless possibilities for experimenting present themselves as you become more proficient. Beginners however, would do well to confine themselves to wool and the following range of fleeces is recommended for hand spinners.

Herdwick	harsh
Romney	medium
Masham	medium
Cheviot	medium
Shropshire	medium
Lleyn	medium
Kerry Hill	medium
Beulah Speckled Face	medium
Jacobs	soft
Shetland Cross	soft
Welsh Mountain Black	soft

Within any breed of sheep there is always considerable variation in the fleeces. The characteristic to look for in selecting a fleece for hand-spinning are the staple length[1] of 10-15cm and thickness or count[2] of about 45's-60's, and a soft medium or harsh handle dependent on the thread's eventual use. In addition hand-spinners are always appreciative of clean fleeces free from vegetable matter and fleeces with unusual colour patterns.

The wool marketing board runs a special service for hand-spinners and will send you a leaflet giving details and prices of fleeces available from year to year.

[1] Wool fibres come in locks called 'staple'.
[2] Wool fibres are found in varying degrees of thickness. This is assessed by a count which is the number of hanks (560 yards) of yarn which can be spun from 1lb of wool. The finer the wool, the greater the length of the yarn for the same weight.

USEFUL INFORMATION

Suppliers of Fleece

British Wool Marketing Board
Oak Mills, Clayton, Bradford, West Yorkshire, BD14 6JD. (Variety of fleeces.)

Eliza Leadbetter
Rookery Cottage, Daleford, Lane Whitegate, Northwich, Cheshire. (Variety of fleeces and fibres.)

Lesley Kilbride
Arrina, Strathcarron, W. Ross, Scotland. (Shetland/Gotland fleeces.)

Spinning and Weaving Materials and Equipment

Eliza Leadbetter
Address as above. (Wide range of equipment for spinners and weavers.)

Handweaver's Studio and Gallery Ltd.
29 Haroldstone Road, London, E17 7AN. (Spinning and weaving equipment—studio space and instruction.)

Dryad Crafts
P.O. Box 38, Northgates, Leicester, LE1 9BU. (All craft supplies, including spinning and weaving.)

Spinning Wheels

Frank Herring
27 High West Street, Dorchester. (Spinning wheels and spinning accessories.)

Haldane & Co. (Woodturners) Ltd.
Gateside, Fife, Scotland, KY14 7ST. (Spinning wheels and cards.)
Timber Top Tables Co.
97 Lonsdale Road, Thurmaston, Leicester, LG4 8JJ. (Spinning wheels and cards.)

Yarns

Texere Yarns
9 Peckover Street, Bradford, BD15 BD. (Wide variety of yarns specially produced for handloom weaving.)
Hyslop & Bathgate & Co.
Victoria Works, Galashiels, Scotland. (Looms for handloom weaving.)
Weavers Shop
Royal Wilton Carpet Factory, Wilton, Wiltshire. (Carpet yarns and thrums.)
J. McAndrew Road Mills, Queens Road, Halifax. (Yarns for handloom weaving.)

List of Tools

Saws
20'' hacksaw, 10 points to 1''
10'' tenon saw, 14 points to 1''
Junior hacksaw
Coping saw

Screw Drivers
12'' straight
6'' straight

Hammer
Claw, 16 oz

Mallet
Wooden

Surforms
10'' straight and ½'' round

Chisels
¾'', ½'', ¼''

Set Square
6''

Ruler
Metal, metric

Brace
Rachet

Bits
¼'', ½'', ¾'' adjustable large and countersunk

Drill
Hand

Files
Small round
9'' straight bastard cut
Small triangular

Glue
Wood workers glue
Araldite

Varnish
Clear

Sandpaper
Assorted

Vice and Workbench

Book Suppliers

K. R. Drummond
30 Hart Grove, London, W5. (Books on weaving and textiles. Mail order only.)
Pantiles Book Shop
Tonbridge Wells, Kent. (Books on textiles, weaving and spinning.)

Further Reading

MAGAZINES

Weavers Journal, c/o Federation of British Craft Societies, 43 Earlham Street, London, WC2. (Quarterly magazine devoted to hand-spinning, hand-weaving and dyeing.)

SHEEP

British Sheep Breeds (British Wool Marketing Board).
Sheepkeeping on a Small Scale by Edward Hart (Thorsons Publishers, Wellingborough).

SPINNING

Handspinning by Eliza Leadbetter (Cassell, London).

Spinning Wool, a leaflet (Dryad Press, London).

WEAVING

The Techniques of Weaving by John Tovey (Batsford, London).

Weaving by Znamceroski (Pan Books, London).

The Weaver's Craft by Simpson and Weir (Dryad Press, London).

Practical Four Shaft Weaving by Vera Miles (Dryad Press, London).

INDEX